I0762749

The Gardener's Mindset

Climbing rose 'Crown Princess Margareta'.

The Gardener's Mindset

Connecting with Nature through Plants

Text and photographs by Stephen Orr

Illustrations by Chad Jacobs

Clarkson Potter/Publishers

New York

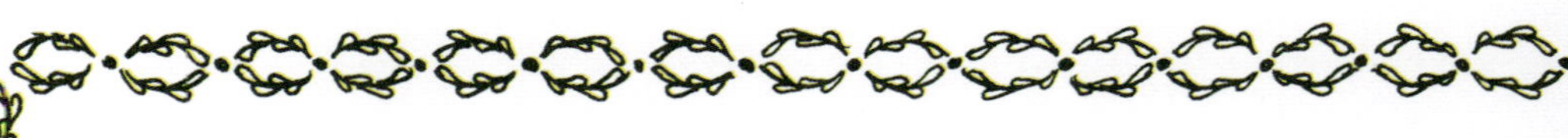

CONTENTS

LESSONS

A collection of
heirloom hyacinths.

INTRODUCTION

My garden exists mostly deep within my brain. When I first started gardening in earnest in my twenties, I was hungry to find out everything I could about the topic. I thought that garden encyclopedias or how-to manuals would be the best source of knowledge. However, over those first years I was surprised to learn that a certain genre of books—garden essays—gave me so much more. These writings by twentieth-century authors, such as Thalassa Cruso, Elizabeth Lawrence, Henry Mitchell, Mirabel Osler, Eleanor Perényi, Michael Pollan, and Vita Sackville-West, taught me not only *how* to garden but how to *think* about gardening. Through them, I not only gained practical knowledge about horticulture but also absorbed abstract concepts like taste, style, and historical lore. I still keep stacks of these books on my nightstand as inspiration. They are a pleasure to read before bedtime and much more centering for my mental health than poking at my phone.

Today, when people want a horticultural answer, they search online for their specific gardening problems. While these sources are effective, they're also transactional in a way that can deprive the gardener of the chance to discover something new and unexpected. The essays in this book are an analog counterpoint to today's algorithmically derived online media. The act of reading a book gives us a much-needed

'Seaside Swirl' rugosa roses mingle with 'Apricot Beauty' foxgloves and Sicilian honey garlic (*Allium siculum*).

respite from our phones, which have become the default we reach for instantly when we have an in-between moment to browse.

As with those works by the authors I mention above, this collection of essays explores my relationship to plants but more importantly nature, pulling from the four gardens my husband and I have created over the past decades. I want to highlight the emotional sense of well-being a gardener can experience while digging in the soil. Our gardens are that rare space where we can enter a state of creative flow and allow our thoughts to run. I hope to inspire more people to enjoy the offline pleasures of gardening as a refuge from technology and current events. But also, I want to entice them to engage with nature and reclaim some of the time they may have given over to the agitation of social media. Gardening improves not only our physical health but our mental health as well by helping to cut down on distractions and foster focus. I want to encourage the power that comes with merely sitting and observing the sheer wonder of plants whether they are in the woods, the sand dunes, or right in your own backyard.

Gardening should be an act of joy, but what I hear most from new gardeners is—trepidation. They worry about making a mistake, a fatal one because it involves killing a plant. Though I hate to waste my gardening budget, I have learned the most from what did not go as planned: the clematis I pruned at the wrong time, the houseplants I drowned, or the all-you-can-eat hosta buffet I generously provided to the local deer population. When things do not work out the way seed packets say they will, beginner gardeners often give up. Why not instead give yourself a little grace and view failure as a learning opportunity? Research the reasons something did not go well while observing nature's lessons on how to avoid it from happening again.

***

The idea for this type of thought-inducing gardening book was born in the early part of the pandemic. My husband Chad and I spent that first year of lockdown in our apartment in Queens just minutes from the COVID epicenter of Elmhurst Hospital. The fear, stress, and unscheduled hours of those early days caused many people to reevaluate their lives. What are we doing and why? Our first getaway, once things cleared up a bit that initial summer, was to Cape Cod, a place of singular natural beauty where, through a series of chance meetings and luck, we decided to buy a house. It was—and is—a big stretch for us in every way, but it has truly turned out to be our happy place.

Making a garden at the Cape has been a challenge. But there have also been pluses. I fell in love with the resilient types of plants that grow well in our lean, sandy, seaside conditions—especially such Mediterranean plants as bearded iris, catmint, lavender, rosemary, sage, and thyme. I admire them for their scrappiness in the face of our dramatic storms. We are on the narrowest part of the Cape peninsula where some days I can hear the Atlantic ocean swells crashing on one side, and on others I can hear the waves hitting the opposing bay beaches. But the changing climate also brings more drought, as our spring seasons seem to be getting increasingly drier. The native plants we enjoy on our hikes through the Cape Cod National Seashore, such as scrub oak, white oak, serviceberries, wild bluberries, beach plums, sweetfern, and bayberry, are beautiful on their own. But I have also expanded my horticultural palette by bringing in soil and compost to create a richer environment for a kitchen garden and several flower borders of annuals and perennials. Now in our fourth year here, we are finding success on many levels, while at the same time, wondering what happened with certain plants.

This book is not only about our current garden. I also share the lessons I've learned from our past gardens in Manhattan, upstate New York, and Des Moines, Iowa, and through my experience as an author of garden books and editor at brands such as *Better Homes & Gardens, Domino, House & Garden, Martha Stewart Living,* and *The New York Times.* I always consider the experience of American gardeners nationwide, from Maine to California. It's not easy to handle every situation—that will be for each gardener to experience and figure out—but I try to keep any lesson geographically adaptable. Every garden I have tended has yielded distinct lessons, in conditions ranging from coastal/waterwise to woodland/deer-plagued and in settings from urban/containers to suburban clay soil/shade.

In its present state, my Cape Cod garden is far from a showplace, though I may make it look appealing on Instagram with good light and carefully chosen camera angles. My yard functions more as an experimental lab, a space where I can learn through observation the ways plants want to exist in nature. I like to take chances and try things the experts say might be marginally cold hardy or too fragile for our stormy winds. I enjoy seeing a new gardener get a similar horticultural bug and watching them gain confidence over the years. I believe through the personal essay approach, gardeners of all ages can learn from my experiences, both positive and negative. I describe my communication style as opinion-rich, but judgment-free.

As Thomas Jefferson wrote in a letter at the age of sixty-eight, "No occupation is so delightful to me as the culture of the earth, & no culture comparable to that of the garden. . . . the failure of one thing repaired by the success of another. . . . but tho' an old man, I am but a young gardener." I can think of no better way to go through life, with one hand digging in the soil and the other tending a flower. I hope readers of *The Gardener's Mindset* will feel the same as they more closely examine the power gardening possesses to connect human intelligence to nature, serving as a reminder to stop and reflect on our place in an increasingly hectic world. Remember, if you need me, I'll be out in the garden.

Blue camassias against a backdrop of purple alliums and lilacs.

OPPOSITE: Houseplants enjoy the summer heat on the screened porch.

Thoreau once walked the Outer Cape's majestic Back Shore beaches.

Your Garden
The Dry Garden
BETH CHATTO
GARDENING
by
V. SACKVILLE-WEST
THE GARDENER'S BED-BOOK
RICHARDSON WRIGHT
An American Gardener
LOUISE
A GARDENER'S TESTAMENT
THE GARDENER'S WEEK-END BOOK
LONDON
SEELEY SERVICE & Co. Ltd
Margery Fish
WE MADE A GARDEN
Katharine S. White
THE GARDENING YEAR
WITH THE AUTHOR OF "MAKING THINGS GROW" AND "MAKING

OPPOSITE (*clockwise from top left*): In one of my newly planted front beds during Lockdown; a selection of favorite garden books; lilacs planted by the original owner anchor each corner of our Cape house; 'Dalmatian Peach' foxglove.

This vast expanse of dunes was protected as the Cape Cod National Seashore by President Kennedy in 1961.

BULB CRAZY

I'm planting bulbs today. It's a bright but chilly mid-November afternoon and I am exactly where I want to be, sitting on the ground rooting around in the flower beds like a squirrel. Except that unlike a squirrel, I'm putting the bulbs in and not taking them out. I've always been a bulb evangelist, spreading my passion for these cheerful little flowers with friends and acquaintances whenever opportunity arises. If I meet someone who has gardening questions after moving into a new house, I ask them if they've planted bulbs yet. It's the first thing I recommend doing. Bulbs are the easiest way for beginners to get a head start on a new garden. Each arrives as a pre-programmed flower packet ready to bloom its first year, so unless you get a rotten one, success is guaranteed. Planting them is an exercise in hope and patience—executed six months in advance.

I begin my dreaming in midsummer by searching the inventories of my favorite catalogs both online and in print, starting with a long list of narcissus varieties. I'm partial to the old-fashioned scented Jonquilla types of daffodils, the flat-cupped Poeticus class like 'Actaea' and 'Pheasant's Eye', and the peachy-apricot color range. I usually avoid the split-cup hybrids that look odd and mutant, like the hybridizer needed to establish a few more guardrails around what is scientifically possible and what is aesthetically desirable for gardeners. Just because you can . . . but maybe that's me just being

My expanding collection of poppy anemones (*Anemone coronaria*).

conservative. Check back with me in a few years and I might be letting my freak flag fly with a whole flotilla of outrageous split-cups.

I first fell hard for narcissus when we had a lake cabin in upstate New York. I discovered that daffodils are one of the few plants that deer won't eat, so we filled the rough grass in the front yard with hundreds of daffodils over the years. It was an impressive sight to see in April and May as I kept adding more and more. Our small yard was filled with a sea of yellow, orange, peach, and white blossoms that I cut and transported back to the city. When I close my eyes, I can smell that piercingly sweet narcissus scent filling the car. To get the best blooms in subsequent years, we resisted the urge to cut back the leaves until after the flowers faded so the plants could photosynthesize for several weeks. But the resulting yellowing foliage made our yard look a little disheveled by late May. One of our neighbors, a nosy but sweet man who zipped around the neighborhood in a little golf cart keeping tabs on things, would stop by and ask when we were going to deal with the "weeds." My explanation that they were daffodils and that they needed to have their bulbs fed by photosynthesis was met with a blank stare. For some people, a pristine lawn ranks above all else.

Besides my long affair with daffodils, I've also been trying different types of spring anemones over the past several years. I first attempted growing the hardy Grecian or Balkan windflowers (*Anemone blanda*) in Des Moines where temperatures can dive well below zero in winter. Their small daisy flowers arrive in early spring in a narrow range of commercially available colors: blue ('Blue Shades'), white ('White Splendour'), pink ('Pink Star'), and mauve ('Charmer'). They live up to their name as they tremble and nod in the breeze—*ánemos* is Greek for "wind." I try to imagine where my bulbs grow in their natural habitat when I'm planting them because it helps me decide where they would look most at home. They may be imported from Holland, but the original species of the blandas comes from rocky high-altitude spots and alpine meadows of southeastern Europe, Turkey, and the Middle East. I always order many more of the small bulbs than I think I need—a little does not go a long way with these tiny beauties. Blandas did well in Des Moines under an old ash tree as they knit together into large pastel patches about six inches tall, enjoying the sunlight for several weeks before the tree above them leafed out. Last year I put a big group of them in a raised flower bed in our Cape Cod garden edged by a rough outline of stones, which allows them good drainage and a nice visual backdrop. Like many bulbs, they are spring ephemerals. All traces of their foliage will vanish in late June or July, so put them alongside a plant that will come up later and fill in any bare spots.

Last year I took a chance with their more flamboyant cousins, the poppy anemones (*Anemone coronaria*), a flower I've tried to grow in multiple gardens without much success. For years, I optimistically planted them and nothing would happen. They are less cold hardy than blandas and I had feared they wouldn't last through our Cape Cod winters, but because they are listed as Zones 7 to 10 and we recently went from 7A to 7B, I thought I'd give them a try. Success! These weirdly shaped, shrunken tubers I planted the previous autumn sprang up and bloomed for weeks and weeks. Each blossom is a graphic masterpiece; the petals are rounded and large with a distinctive black pincushion of pistils and a ring of stamens in the middle, often surrounded by a white corona that glows like a solar eclipse. They come in two main forms—'De Caen', which are single-petalled, and 'St. Brigid' or 'Fullstar', which are semi-double or double. The most common colors are true blue ('Mr. Fokker'), pink ('Sylphide'), white ('The Bride'), and a bright scarlet ('Governor'). I love them all but have a hard time blending in the red color with the others, though I have seen videos on social media of the wild scarlet species covering Grecian hillsides. Maybe I'll try them by themselves in a grassy patch next year.

Building on my success, this year I scoured the internet and found a new series of poppy anemone hybrids from Italy grouped under the name 'Mistral'. Their subtle colorations and shading look as if they were painted by hand with a watercolor brush. I'm growing them on the northern edge of their hardiness, but two factors might be helping: my sandy soil (these are Mediterranean plants that prefer sharp drainage so they don't rot), and their placement in a flower bed close to the foundation where they'll get heat from my house. One tip from experience: Always soak your anemone tubers in tepid water for several hours before you plant them to give them a little wake-up call.

I used to be ambivalent about hyacinths in the garden. I've always enjoyed these horticultural oddballs as cut flowers or in pots but have avoided planting them outdoors because they look so overbred in most garden settings, almost like the plastic flowers. These are bodacious flowers, top-heavy and prone to flopping in the mud. However, I've found that positioned in my herb garden, sprouting randomly between brick paths and low wattle fencing, they look like the stylized flowers in a medieval tapestry. Somehow the formality of the four-square design helps integrate these oddly unnatural-looking flowers.

It's their strong fragrance that truly draws me in—a mix of honey, sweetcorn, and wisteria. I also admire their colors, ranging from pure white to almost black and with every flower tone between except green; though even that appears at the tips of some hybrids. Hyacinths become more graceful as they age into adulthood. After their first year, when they look fairly stout, they usually return with a slenderer form and fewer blooms that resemble *Hyacinthus orientalis,* the original Mediterranean wildflower, or a Spanish bluebell (*Hyacinthoides hispanica*). I was even more determined to grow hyacinths when I read in an Old House Gardens catalog that they are the most commercially endangered bulbs. Introduced to Europe from Turkey in the sixteenth century, they became so popular that by the early eighteenth century there were more than two thousand hybrids. Now you might find only a dozen or so in the trade. When you plant one, especially if you buy some of the rarer heirloom types, you are preserving its genes for future gardeners. Being someone who enjoys history as well as a bit of a challenge, I bought as many types of hyacinths as I could order from online sources. I ended up finding more than two dozen hybrids with an emphasis on the blues I love so much as well as several of the more unusual hybrids: the near-black 'Dark Dimension', reddish-purple 'Woodstock', double-flowered indigo 'Dreadnought', butter yellow 'City of Haarlem', apricot 'Gypsy Queen', bicolor pink and green 'Rainbow Road UltraDouble', and the dainty (and hard to find) Roman hyacinths that closely resemble the original wildflower species.

In addition to my love for the plants themselves, I enjoy daydreaming about where I will place my bulbs and what they will look like in different areas of the garden. Maybe it's because of my background as a garden editor who worked on a lot of photo shoots, but I plan my garden by thinking of it as a series of pictures. I planted a row of tall purple and white alliums dotting a flower border in an erratic rhythm. I imagine hearing them as a percussive *pop, pop, pop,* bouncing their way through the early summer perennials. I also added tall dark plum fritillaries (*Fritillaria persica*), which fill the gap between the earliest crocuses and the tulips.

I also want to use bulbs in the gravel garden, but the challenge is to pick what will look natural there. Once again, I think about which plants grow in stony, pebbled areas. I wouldn't put a large-cupped hybrid daffodil or a tall, voluptuous tulip in the rock garden—plants there need to look wild. Smaller, delicate flowers seem more at home in gravel. There's something about the contrast between their soft petals and the surrounding stone. Overbred flowers that look too touched by the hand of the hybridizer don't work here. Instead, I will plant miniature daffodils like the hoop petticoat (*Narcissus bulbocodium*) and more restrained-looking hybrids, such as 'Tete-a-Tete'. Graceful species like the lady tulip (*Tulipa clusiana*) and the short-stemmed water lily tulip (*T. kaufmanniana*) also seem at home. Among those, I'll plant as many of the small bulbs as I can afford: crocuses, squills, glory-of-the-snows, winter aconites, and best of all, rock garden irises (*Iris reticulata*) with their many colors and relatively small size, growing only to about four to six inches. Looking up reference photos of their native habitats helps me in creating the right setting, artificial as it is, in my garden. If I didn't already have the sandy soil and the stones, say, maybe a boggy grass area, I'd switch gears and try bulbs that thrive in those conditions. Over the years, I've learned to head where nature guides me.

Start your bulb ordering early so that you get exactly what you want before they sell out. After years of waiting until the last minute, now I order as soon as the companies launch their new lists in the summer. Ordering early, you'll find the unusual varieties that make experimentation so fun. I also recommend holding back a bit of your budget for a final bulb order at the last minute to take advantage of the many clearance sales that occur in late October and even into November. You can get discounts that make your burgeoning bulb order feel a little less extravagant. Or at least that's what I tell myself.

I have a "more is more" philosophy with bulbs—I can't have too many. The limits are, of course, budget, planting time, and labor. However, judging by the size and weight of my recent mail-order deliveries, I seem to fairly easily be able to rationalize overruling those concerns. An explosion of spring flowers that begins in the first sunny days of late winter and lasts for three months or more gives me all the excuse I need to go a little over-the-top with one of my favorite groups of garden plants.

OVERLEAF, LEFT (*clockwise from top left*): *Anemone blanda* with *A. coronaria;* Guinea-hen flower (*Fritillaria meleagris*); snowdrop 'Flore Pleno'; a collection of scented daffodils.

OVERLEAF, RIGHT: Tulips fill the long border in spring.

LESSON

BULBS FOR SPECIFIC LOCATIONS

This is one of the most forgiving groups of plants. The bulbs you buy are raised in optimal conditions and are almost guaranteed to bloom their first year. However, getting them to return and thrive depends on planting them in spots that are conducive to their natural growing environment. Most bulbs prefer sunny, well-drained situations, though many are forgiving of less than ideal conditions. Here are some suggestions for planting bulbs in other spots in your garden.

- For moist conditions: bluebells, camassia, daffodils, fritillaries, snowdrops, star-of-Bethlehem, summer snowflake
- For rock or gravel gardens: alliums, anemones, crocuses, glory-of-the-snow, miniature daffodils, rock garden irises, snowdrops, species tulips, squills
- For lawns: crocuses, daffodils, glory-of-the-snow, grape hyacinths, squills
- For meadows and long grass: alliums, camassia, daffodils
- For shade gardens or woodlands: camassia, colchicum, corydalis, English bluebells, fritillaries, hardy cyclamen, Italian arums, lilies of the valley, snowdrops, squills, star-of-Bethlehem, summer snowflake, trout lilies, winter aconite

PREVIOUS SPREAD: A full spectrum of hyacinth varieties.

THIS PAGE: My mom loved flowers, so gardens were always a big part of my childhood travel. Here I am in front of a clump of Hawaiian bougainvillea in the 1970s.

ROSE-COLORED GLASSES

I carry with me a mental scrapbook of special plants from my childhood. These sensory recollections can pop up suddenly when I catch the scent of lilac on the breeze or see a flash of peony pink while passing in the car. When such memories surface, I try to pause and reflect on the moment that accompanies them: playing hide-and-seek in the neighbor's shrubs on a spring day or riding with my parents to church.

I grew up in the small city of Abilene, Texas. Our street wasn't busy with cars, and we knew the names of every homeowner on the block. The summers were filled with kids roaming here and there without a care, through front yards, over fences, and even occasionally into backyards. We knew from experience which neighbors might give us trouble and tell our parents what we were up to.

When my friends were occupied elsewhere, I'd explore the neighborhood alone. I can still map out the plants I doted on along my West Texas street like it was yesterday. A wisteria trained into a single stem stood at the end of the block, almost like a short stylized tree you'd find in an *Alice in Wonderland* book. When it was in full bloom, I'd spend hours sitting underneath its low branches like I was in my own clubhouse, inhaling the sweet-corn fragrance from the long purple racemes. I also visited the roses on the block, many quite tall and spindly from lack of pruning. I'd ramble around in the summer sun, going on tiptoe, sniffing to check which were scented and which weren't. I can easily imagine a neighbor spotting me from the window and telling their spouse, "George, that Orr boy is in the backyard again." I still find scentless roses a bit disappointing.

In our backyard was a single-petalled pink 'Betty Prior' rose by the back gate, flanked by two old-fashioned bridal wreath bushes (*Spiraea* x *vanhouttei*) that bloomed in a fountain of white froth in May. My dad and I also tended a low row of tiny Polyantha roses in the front beds and a classic 'Chicago Peace' hybrid tea in the back. I remember him telling me all the names of the roses and showing me their tags. Though these plants might be considered ordinary or outdated compared to newer hybrids, for me they hold a sentimental value.

Next to our front steps was a dense patch of red-flowered plants with a spicy, powdery fragrance I found intriguing. I enjoyed cutting the scarlet flowers with their brushy white stripes for the house, though my mom did not exactly enjoy the way the hollow stems dripped water on the carpet when I carried them in. For years, I tried to locate this mystery plant. Although they looked like some sort of frost-tender amaryllis, they were hardy, able to withstand the winter temperatures that could dip into the teens or twenties in our part of Texas. My parents referred to them as daylilies (*Hemerocallis*), but clearly they weren't because they each had a distinct bulb. Years later, thanks to the internet, I found out that it was a St. Joseph's lily (*Hippeastrum* x *johnsonii*), an heirloom variety of amaryllis that had become a pass-along plant in Texas, typically only found in older gardens. Once when I was in my twenties and I'd returned to Texas for a visit to see my parents, I dug up a patch of the bulbs and transported them in a carry-on bag to NYC. I grew them in my apartment as a potted houseplant for a few years before they petered out.

Several houses on my West Texas block were distinctive because they avoided ordinary suburban foundation shrub plantings and tidy green lawns. One front yard featured what we'd now call a xeriscape or dry garden composed of crushed white rock, red yuccas, and silver santolina. I remember the tactile sensation of the little yellow pincushion santolina flowers when I'd crush them in my hand on the way to school. Most significantly, I recall their scent, which was acrid and bitter but pleasantly reminiscent of the desert not so many miles to the west of us. Currently, I grow half a dozen santolina in my Cape garden, and their scent evokes memories of those original plants every time I sniff them. Botanical fragrances have always been big triggers for me as mnemonic devices, not so surprising since the sense of smell is one of the most primitive of our senses, hardwired in our forebrain.

Though my dad didn't consider himself much of a gardener, he greatly influenced my interests as a young child. He often took me for after-dinner walks on spring evenings to pick wildflowers, usually just the two of us. Texas wildflowers are in a class by themselves. The pungent smell of the blanket flowers, bluebonnets, coreopsis, evening primroses, paintbrushes, and sand verbenas we gathered to bring home takes me back to those days. And yes, we picked wildflowers back then—we didn't know any better. They were ostensibly for my mom, but I suspect I might've treasured them even more. I made flower arrangements for her all spring and summer, sometimes from fields by the highway or from our garden, or sometimes from a neighbor's yard.

Across the street from us lived an elderly couple with the wonderfully anachronistic names of Overton and Sybil Faubus who enjoyed the act of gardening more than most of our other neighbors. I can picture them—Mrs. Faubus in her capri pants and bejeweled glasses, and Mr. Faubus always gentlemanly in his wide-brimmed ranch hat and khaki coveralls. During growing season, I'd often be at their side "helping out" while they worked. Their pristine lawn was the finest in the neighborhood and they did not like us kids playing on it, particularly with games like swinging statue or red rover that involved a lot of running and skidding on the turf. The Faubuses had the first hydrangeas and lilacs I'd ever seen. Whether they realized it or not, they were my mentors as knowledgeable gardeners familiar with the names of the plants they were growing. The reverence and care they gave their gardens let me know that what they were growing was special, even if fairly common. Recently, I started growing the old-fashioned annual balsam impatiens (also known as touch-me-nots) in memory of the Faubuses, who first demonstrated to me how the spring-loaded seeds exploded when pinched. Being rampant self-seeders, these plants have now popped up all over my vegetable garden, but I don't mind. They're easy to remove.

At this point you might be wondering, Did this kid have friends? Yes, I did, thank you for asking. I was part of a gang of children on the block. During summer breaks, we'd meet up at a particular group of tall sycamores that served as our skyscraper meeting place during summer breaks. We usually climbed them as a group, each of us sitting on our preferred branch in the largest tree, which I had named Zeus after developing an obsession with my older sister's Greek mythology schoolbook by Edith Hamilton. Over the course of several summers, I ended up naming most of the larger trees on the block. Hera was naturally the large sycamore next to her husband Zeus. Poseidon was another tall tree located in my friend's backyard with his wife Amphitrite next to him. Apollo and Artemis were two silvery pecan trees that were beautiful to look at but uncomfortable to climb with their rough bark. If any adults were paying attention in those days, they must've thought it odd to see a group of eight-year-olds running down the street proclaiming, "I'm climbing Zeus! I've got dibs on Poseidon!"

Our parents would have been horrified to know how far we'd clambered up those trees. I recall several instances when my friends and I climbed high into a fifty-foot sycamore, feeling it sway wildly in the winds of an approaching West Texas thunderstorm. Reflecting on it now, I feel a sense of fear in the pit of my stomach, but I didn't feel afraid then. Like most young people, then and now, we were shielded by our naivety and sense of invincibility. What a thrill those climbs were as we screamed and laughed, the wind buffeting us as we perched precariously in Zeus's upper branches and clutched the trunk. Only the onset of the first heavy raindrops and flashes of lightning would compel us to finally come to our senses and scramble down like silly monkeys.

The lesson? Our parents never knew a thing. We're all still here, and I continue to have an enduring fondness for sycamores and their smooth, velvety branches.

PENTHOUSE SERENADE

In the 1990s, we lived in a duplex penthouse on West Nineteenth Street in Manhattan. That sounds swankier than it actually was, seeing how there were three of us twentysomething, entry-level professionals living in a very small amount of square footage. In the rest of the country, a duplex usually means two living units positioned side by side in a house. In New York City, it indicates an apartment with two floors. Ours was basically two rooms, one on top of the other. Chad and I were upstairs while our friend Barbara was downstairs in an alcove that had been sectioned off into a bedroom. We often referenced the theme from *Three's Company* and it was definitely tight, but we made it work for several years before Barbara moved to Los Angeles and Chad and I could finally afford the rent.

What really made the apartment livable was the sliding glass door in our bedroom that led to a rooftop space. It too was nothing fancy, just a tar paper surface, a ladder up to the building's wooden water tower, and a brick parapet. But it did have several key features in its favor. The space was relatively large, around five hundred square feet, with wide-open views of the Empire State Building and Chrysler Building on one side and the Hudson River and High Line (long before it was a park) on the other. Most importantly, there was an outdoor faucet to hook up a hose. I immediately knew I wanted to make a garden there. First up was a small window box I filled with herbs bought at the farmers' market. Over the next fourteen years, bit by bit, Chad and I made an extensive garden of various containers—adding pots, soil, garden furniture, and hundreds of plants. Each item, large or small, was pulled into the elevator and hoisted up the last flight of stairs to the rooftop door, often step by step with rests in between. The largest was an eight-foot, balled-and-burlapped birch tree.

We became obsessed with our garden. I wanted to learn as much as I could about horticulture in general, so I started reading garden magazines and books by great authors from the past and present. I went to all the garden lectures I could find. If there had been a consumer-facing internet in those days, I would have combed it as well. I spent most of my spare time—when I wasn't at my job as a magazine graphic designer—either gardening or going down an analog version of a horticultural rabbit hole. Soon, I got deeply into roses and clematis, both of which were very popular in the Anglophilic late 1980s and early '90s. I read Graham Stuart Thomas for Old Rose knowledge and planted as many Madames as I could: magenta climber 'Mme. Isaac Pereire', cream-colored 'Mme. Alfred Carrière', and pristine white 'Mme. Hardy'.

I grew dozens of clematis, including my first love, the deep purple 'Jackmanii'. It was the first clematis I had ever seen—covering the pole where I parked my bicycle at my childhood piano teacher's house. I also grew lavender-colored 'Comtesse de Bouchaud', pink-striped 'Nelly Moser', large white 'Henryi', and dark red 'Niobe'. I made trellises for them out of long, straight ailanthus branches, the weed trees that grew in the abandoned lot behind our building. At first, I grew simple annual vines, such as morning glories and moonflowers. Then I got more adventurous with hummingbird vine, silver lace vine, sweet autumn clematis, and cobaea, the exotic purple or white cup-and-saucer-vine from Central and South America that manages to hit full bloom right as frost arrives.

Though we were both interested in working in the garden, my new hobby really started to take over my interests, as well as our apartment. After Barbara moved away, I took over the downstairs bathroom—thankfully we had two—and started seeds in the bathtub with a four-foot grow light perched precariously on the rim. After falling hard for tender perennials and herbs, I overwintered my rosemary, night-blooming cestrum, calamondin orange, and Meyer lemons in the living room. I kept reading and acquiring. Not one to be held back by the reality that I wasn't gardening in the ground, I added shrubs, such as hydrangeas, caryopteris, clethra, and lilacs, as well as tall trees, such as river birch, several types of cherries, and Japanese maples. Everything was in pots, with the largest being about thirty inches wide. The trees grew fifteen feet tall; the vines scrambled up the trellises. I planned a sequence of blooms from early spring bulbs to the last asters and the occasional China rose at Christmas. I was a young man with the rare chance to garden in NYC, and I was in heaven.

We bought a dining table and an outdoor couch at a West Village secondhand shop. The rooftop was an idyllic place to lounge or read a book. I tried sleeping out under the stars a couple of times, which was pretty blissful as I nodded off, even if it was to the sound of the nearby air-conditioning units, the beeps of distant traffic, and the dull rumble of planes flying up the west side of Manhattan to LaGuardia. White flowers I planted to catch the half light of the city's illumination, including two standard Peegee hydrangeas on either side, gave me a sense of privacy. However, I never made it through a whole night out there. I always woke up chilly around four a.m., feeling a bit exposed and unsafe. It was, after all, a garden in the middle of a giant city, flanked by taller buildings on one side, which I had become accustomed to ignoring, sometimes to my detriment.

One afternoon, as I bent over untangling a clematis from a trellis, I felt a sharp pain in my rear and saw a little ball from a pellet gun roll away. Like the true New Yorker I was becoming, and not wanting to give my neighbor the pleasure of knowing they'd scored a direct hit, I made my way calmly inside without glancing up. I hoped it was just a kid pulling a prank and, thankfully, it never happened again. On another even more unnerving occasion, when the lock to the public door to the roof was broken, someone began to jiggle the latch on our sliding door at two a.m. Fortunately, we had a metal pole in its track. Seeing the human shadow against the closed blinds, I jumped out of bed and in the deepest, butchest voice I could summon in the middle of the night I shouted, "Get out of here! I have a gun!" The figure froze and then casually walked to the door and down the stairs. In those days in 1990s NYC, we didn't even call the police because that's just the way things were. PS: I was bluffing about the gun.

Negative moments like that were few and far between, but as my plant mania grew, I did begin to feel a slow-growing sense of guilt about the weight restrictions for the rooftop. We had not asked anyone for permission to put a garden up on the ninth floor, and by anyone, I mean the landlord. When savvier guests asked about such pesky details, I distracted them by plucking a star jasmine blossom for them to sniff. I was in denial. Our building was not very well run. The nondescript redbrick building was built in the 1980s and '90s with cheap sliding windows and Fedder air-conditioning panels on the outside. These structures were so ubiquitous they earned the epithet Fedder Houses. "So ugly and bland are those buildings, say some, that their most striking architectural trait may well be the air conditioner sleeve itself," wrote reporter Jotham Sederstrom in a 2005 Brooklyn newspaper article.

In a recurring nightmare, I was jolted out of bed by a loud series of crashes and walked outside through the sliding door to see that the roof had collapsed from the weight of all my plants. Each floor collapsed down on the other so that I could peer down the wide, dark hole with plants and flowers, and water dripping down the sides of each layer like subtropical vines dangling in a cenote. I woke up with a start, felt relieved, and then headed off to the garden center to buy more plants the next morning. Once again, pure denial.

Our garden was a haven for us in the concrete maze of Manhattan. On midsummer evenings after work, we watered, which took a long time with all those pots. The residual heat rose off the buildings as the air cooled down and I splashed around and watered in my bare feet, dancing to whichever song of the summer was booming out of a passing Jeep's speakers. The smell of tuberose and Oriental lilies wafted in as the sun set over the Hudson. We hosted many memorable parties up there, both blowouts with dancing, and smaller dinner parties. We enjoyed the polite type of big city voyeurism that Alfred Hitchcock captured so evocatively, idly observing the daily habits of our neighbors in the big building across the street and watching their parties. In that tacit agreement that all New York neighbors have, if I ever saw them on the street, I would look blankly in the other direction.

But all good things come to an end. Fourteen years in, the landlord notified us he was not renewing our lease so that a "family member" could move in. We were bereft. We had built our paradise in the sky on borrowed land. My second worst fear (after a building collapse) had come true. We had a moving sale for friends and co-workers who enthusiastically cleared everything out. The trees, lilacs, roses, containers, and furniture found new homes in other parts of the city. For years, friends sent me updates on the Joe-Pye weed that towered over their East Village backyard, or the 'President Lincoln' lilac that covered itself with Wedgwood blue each May in Brooklyn Heights. That made me happy. Our next apartment, a walk-up on Tenth Avenue with no outdoor space, did not. I knew I had been spoiled by the little aerie we had lucked into and that most city dwellers never got the luxury of having a space to garden. But still.

A few years later, we were able to locate another place to make a garden—this time in the ground. A tiny lake house upstate that had a small quarter-acre plot to garden among the hemlocks, deer, and ferns—and this one we would own without the constant low-grade anxiety of an unrenewed lease, being shot in the rear, or an impending structural collapse. That rooftop housed not only the first garden I could call my own, but it also gave me the passion and education that would lead to a career writing about gardens around the world.

LESSON

CONTAINER GARDENING TIPS

Over my years of rooftop gardening, I was able to create a beautifully planted space with banks of pots arranged to resemble in-ground flower borders. I was proud of what I accomplished so I bristled when a visitor would ask me if I missed having a "real" garden. Containers aren't just for urban gardeners who lack space or terra firma. I find the flexibility and design opportunities they provide to be indispensible, and I include them in any space I garden. Here are some tips I've learned along the way.

- Plants in pots generally do better when arranged in groups because they support one another in a shared environment that retains more moisture. To create a "border" and to achieve different levels for viewing the flowers, I use a choir riser technique. I arrange rows of plants, raising the back row on several upside-down containers that are concealed by lower groupings in the front.

- Watering is the most important task to keep up with when gardening in pots. In some climates, daily watering will be required in midsummer. Larger containers are easier to maintain than smaller ones because the latter, no matter how adorable, dry out very quickly in summer heat.

- Because the water runs through them so readily, containers will need more fertilizer than an in-ground plant. I recommend organic fertilizers like fish or seaweed emulsion but use even those as sparingly as possible.

- Drainage is important to avoid root rot. Never use pots that don't have adequate drainage holes. Depending on the material, you can drill holes or add more if needed. Keep any broken terra-cotta pots to use as drainage shards in the bottom.

- Never use soil from your garden in containers. It doesn't drain properly. Buy, or create your own potting mix.

- For very large pots, many sources recommend using Styrofoam packing peanuts as filler in the bottom, but this can lead to microplastic runoff as well as problems when you go to repot and the plant's roots have wound inextricably around the peanuts. Leftover upside-down plastic nursery pots can be used to take up room but avoid using mulch as a fill-in because it degrades quickly and can block drainage.

- Ceramic or terra-cotta pots allow plants to breathe more than plastic. In cold winter areas, ceramic pots need protection to avoid cracking. For annual plantings, I empty mine of all soil and store them in a shed or porch. For perennial plantings, I move the pot into a covered porch, shed, or unheated garage where they will have dormant temperatures but not freeze entirely. The main way to avoid damage is to not let the pot freeze onto the ground surface; the freezing and thawing will crack the ceramic material.

OVERLEAF: Scrapbook Polaroids show my first garden on a Manhattan rooftop.

MAGENTA THE MALIGNED

In all my gardening experience I have met only one person who confessed admiration for this colour and I have come across but one garden writer who boldly put down in print his admiration for it. Indeed, nearly every writer upon garden topics pauses in his praise of other flower colours to give the despised one a rap in passing. Mr. Bowles writes of 'that awful form of floral original sin, magenta'; Miss Jekyll calls it 'malignant magenta'; and Mrs. Earle, usually so sympathetic and tender toward all flowers, says that even the word magenta, seen often in the pages of her charming book, 'makes the black and white look cheap.'

—Louise Beebe Wilder,
Colour in My Garden (1918)

American garden writer Louise Beebe Wilder's 1918 book, *Colour in My Garden*, is a classic I read decades ago when I had my container garden on a rooftop in Chelsea and did not place much emphasis on color schemes. I merely bought the plants I liked and when a combination occurred that I didn't care for, I rearranged the pots until I achieved a more pleasing visual effect. I was constantly moving things around. However, now that I have a larger amount of space to garden and my plants are firmly rooted in the ground, such swift adjustments are not as simple.

The pristine beauty of 'Rubinato' cosmos.

Color-scheming the garden is harder than I previously thought. Gardeners must contend with imprecise flower descriptions and potentially misleading photographs in online catalogs. In addition, they quickly begin to realize that creating a color-coordinated sequence of blooms is as changeable as the weather (and heavily influenced by it as well when it comes to timing). What I plan in my mind's eye—an eye I would describe as hopelessly optimistic—doesn't always work out the way I envision. For many gardeners, such missteps can lead to disappointment.

Last summer, I carefully planned my fall bulb orders for a well-choreographed, three-month parade of winter aconite, crocuses, anemones, hyacinths, daffodils, and tulips. The following spring started out beautifully with the whites, yellows, and blues one would expect early in the season. Then the daffodils followed up harmoniously in their own warm shades of yellows, whites, peaches, pinks, and oranges—impossible to mess that up. However, trouble followed—my tulips showed up way before I had anticipated, and their colors threw everything off.

Due to the difficulties I've encountered in previous gardens, I remain a tulip novice. My rooftop was too windy and exposed, and the deer in upstate New York and Des Moines would've eaten them to a nub. On the Cape, growing tulips is not a problem because we don't seem to be frequented by deer, maybe due to the local coyotes that keep their numbers low. I've only seen one deer in three years. Influenced by my friend British garden author Sarah Raven I went all in for my tulip order that year and planned a selection of richly toned varieties that would bloom for weeks. She calls her color scheme "boiled sweets," a combination of mauves, maroons, pinks, oranges, lime greens, and dark purples. Though stylish looking on their own, my tulips landed unhappily in the middle of my bright yellow daffodils. "Um, what is happening in the front beds color-wise?" my husband asked one spring morning. "It's not working." And he was right. My color scheme had turned out to be more of an unfounded conspiracy theory. It was not making any sense. To fix the problem for the following year, I decided to banish the daffodils from the tulip beds and move them to the backyard where they can be as yellow as they want to be.

Certain colors blend effortlessly. Grouping cool shades together and handling the warm tones separately often yields good results. As easy as that approach is, it can get a little boring, especially for a gardener like me who is interested in experimenting rather than achieving perfect outcomes. I enjoy playing with colors that other people might be prejudiced against. Some people hate orange flowers—I favor them. As the Louise Beebe Wilder quote at the opening of this essay elucidates, gardeners in the early twentieth century had an aversion to magenta perhaps because of its association with an inexpensive synthetic aniline dye that had been developed in the 1850s. The intense shade of pink was, by the late nineteenth century, perceived to be cheap and overly assertive. The authors that Wilder mentions in *Colour in My Garden*—E. A. Bowles, Gertrude Jekyll, and Alice Morse Earle—were all tastemakers of their time and, for them, magenta was forbidden. Wilder, on the other hand, endorsed the misunderstood shade. She emphasized using it contextually with other colors that can support and highlight its strong tones. As someone who thinks there are no bad colors, just colors used badly, I agree with Louise.

"The best colours to associate with magenta are deeper and paler tones of itself," she advised. She also suggested pairing it with the softening effects of pale blues and whites. I'll admit that strong pinks have always been a challenging color group for me. Eager to experiment this past summer, I tried out what I would call vibratory tones. Just as Wilder had advised so long ago, it is true that magenta combines well with hues close to it on the color wheel—but I wanted to pump them up a bit more so they vibrate in the eye. Consider these plants together: magenta and burgundy dahlias, lilac 'Blue Horizon' ageratum, electric blue *Salvia uliginosa,* and purple asters and verbena. These flowers buzzing near the high-frequency, ultraviolet edge of the spectrum is far more exciting—isn't it?—than a subdued pastel palette.

In a similar vein, I appreciate incorporating magenta on the hotter end of the scale. I think of these as David Hicks colors. The late British decorator was renowned for the bold décor he created for his clients during the 1960s and '70s, applying vibrant fields of color and pattern to carpets, drapes, and walls. The palette I most associate with him includes another vibratory one, in its dynamic combo of magentas, oranges, reds, and golds from the longer wave, near-infrared end of the spectrum. Relying on a tightly edited collection of hot colors or cool colors is a bit risky if the timing goes awry. This year I selected only warm-colored dahlias for my long border, but they bloomed quite late, resulting in a sea of green leaves for longer than I would have liked.

Too often when we discuss garden color schemes, we focus on the flowers, but it's the foliage that occupies most of the space in flower beds. Next year, I intend to be more strategic by incorporating more non-green foliage. Flowers are fleeting, but leaves provide a summer-long constant. For a hot-toned border, I want to add brown and burgundy foliage like dark-leaved dahlias and *Anthriscus sylvestris* 'Ravenswing'. On the other side of the house, silver foliage like artemisia and cardoon will update a palette of pastel blues, mauves, and purples. Establishing a strong amount of leaf color will create a visual baseline if the flower bloom times don't go as planned.

Beyond foliage color, another concept often overlooked by gardeners is the play of light throughout the day. Some colors appear bleak and washed out in the midday sun, while others fade in the evening or tend to glow. White is ideal for a garden meant to be enjoyed at twilight or in the moonlight, but blue also starts to glow at dusk. An analogous phenomenon occurs for scuba divers in the tropics. The vibrant colors of corals and fish they view near the surface become murkier the deeper the divers go, even in crystal clear water. The same principle holds true in gardens as the sun sets. Colors fade in the order they appear in the spectrum, with longer frequencies (reds and oranges) disappearing first. As that happens, blue and violet tones become more pronounced and appear to glow. A nerdy sidenote about magenta: It does not exist in the linear color spectrum because it would fall between red, the longest wavelength, and purple, the shortest. Our brains combine the two to create the bright pink color that somehow we all agree we're seeing. When planning a garden, it's helpful to consider these gloaming effects and where you might find yourself at certain times of day. If you dine outdoors after sunset, pale blue and white flowers will catch your eye and illuminate the area around a terrace or patio better than reds and oranges.

To me, it can be overwhelming when the only color scheme in a garden can best be described as "all of them." While I respect that a gardener might say, "I just love color!" my response would be, "But can you please be more specific?" A clear point of view in any creative endeavor is crucial, be it music, art, or writing. What message are you trying to convey with color? Are you aiming for excitement or tranquility? Because you can't do both. Although I don't have a property-wide color plan, I want each visually connected area to have a cohesive relationship. This is why garden separators like hedges or walls are so important. Without them, the entire space could easily appear chaotic and disorganized.

Much as I'm sounding like a color martinet, I like to challenge myself and explore different tastes. I recognize that pink makes me uncomfortable, maybe because of its sweet and childlike cultural associations. However, some interesting pink plants have found their way into my garden, such as *Verbascum* 'Jackie in Pink' and the outlandishly peachy-pink bearded iris 'Beverly Sills' that resembles the color of a ruffly silk dress that might have been worn by its opera star namesake in the 1980s. These plants have prompted me to challenge my prejudices and even design a pink-forward garden, adding a range of other sherbet tones: apricot, clementine, mango, melon, papaya, and peach (it's interesting how they're all fruit names). I think it might make a successful visual statement to see all those flower colors mixed with a bit of silver and dark plum foliage to mitigate any Barbie-level sweetness.

"No occupation known to me is so absorbing as the distributing and arranging of flowers in the garden with a view to creating beautiful pictures," wrote Louise Beebe Wilder. They don't call it a color "scheme" for nothing. The process of visualizing, planning, and adjusting over months and years takes patience and observation. But that's the fun of gardening. Trying your best with the information at hand, failing or succeeding, and then moving on to the next year both a little bit wiser and a lot more color coordinated.

LESSON

KEEPING TRACK OF COLOR SCHEMES

It can be challenging to maintain a cohesive plant palette in your garden over time. Use these strategies to keep your flower beds looking harmonious.

- Photograph your garden on a regular basis to reference in future years as the plants grow or die. The embedded date information will help you determine when certain plants bloomed.
- When the garden is at peak bloom, and you are happy with the color scheme, pick flowers and leaves and lay them down on a neutral surface. Take a photo of the arrangement and keep it in your phone for easy reference. This will be your goal palette.
- When you're plant shopping online, download images of the varieties you're considering and put them in a folder so that you can open them all at once and see how the color palette is working.
- Go analog by keeping the plant tags you buy and paste them on pieces of paper in a folder or in a notebook to easily remind yourself of what you've purchased in previous seasons.
- Sketch out your preferred plant palette for each flower bed with color pencils or markers and keep it in a notebook, on a bulletin board, or in a phone photo so that you can reference it easily.
- If you are uncomfortable making color choices, stick to hues that live next to one another on the color wheel. Warms with warms. Cools with cools, etc. And don't forget about that base of all-important foliage color.

A late-summer photo laydown can help get a handle on a potential color scheme for next year.

OPPOSITE: Vibrant colors that sit close to one another on the color wheel create a visual dynamism.

A bouquet reveals potential color palettes for the garden.

FROM THE DEVONIAN

There was a time on Earth when there was no soil. The continents were arranged in mega-continents, primarily in the Southern Hemisphere. Their surface was stone, including what is scientifically referred to as the Old Red Sandstone. This was a vast expanse of barren rock that covered most of what later became our present Northern Hemisphere. During the Devonian Period, 419.2 million years ago to 358.9 million years ago, the surface of the land began to green as tiny primitive spore-bearing plants started their tentative foray out of the water and onto land. They clung at first to the stony margins at the ocean's edge, their hairy stems still partially submerged in the water. As these mosses and ferns evolved and thrived, they moved inland. The weathering action of their roots broke up rocks and their bodies' death and subsequent decay left behind organic matter. These combined to form nascent soils that in turn built up over millions of years and finally, by the Middle Devonian, the Earth was covered with forests and soil that could be several feet deep.

This broad oversimplification is a synthesis of what I recently learned about this transitional epoch on one of my favorite radio shows/podcasts, the BBC's *In Our Time*. The main topic of the program was the tetrapod transition that occurred when marine creatures with fins evolved into land animals with feet. The guests, three professors of biology and paleontology, mentioned the formation of soil on Earth as a sidebar. I had not known there had ever been a period on our planet without soil. As host to all terrestrial life for hundreds of millions of years, I thought it had always been there.

Gardeners need to know what type of soil they have to be able to garden successfully. But most people don't really pay attention. They buy plants that they drop into the "dirt," dosing them with generic fertilizers whether the plants require them or not. My first in-ground garden in upstate New York was on very heavy clay. I used to joke that we should open a pottery workshop because the consistency of our native soil was more like earthenware clay than growing material. We did our best to improve it with compost and soil amendments, but it never made much difference. I had a friend in the neighborhood who later moved out to the North Fork of Long Island where the soil is an enviable sandy loam. She confessed afterward that she always thought she was a terrible gardener until she got there. It was the heavy upstate soil that had foiled her.

Besides being heavy and full of clay, the Sullivan County soil where our cabin was located was also very stony, making planting difficult. I spent thousands of dollars on plants that never made it, either because of poor soil conditions or deer. So we began growing what was already thriving around us in nature. Like proper Devonians, we moved moss and dozens of ferns around our property, particularly the native ostrich ferns that transplanted easily. We grew foxgloves, daffodils, and any other poisonous plants deer won't touch. Ultimately, I went back to growing most of my plants in containers so that I could give them the soil they needed to thrive. If we had lived there longer, I'm sure I could have composted my way out of the situation over time. Good compost is a gardener's panacea.

The soil in my Des Moines garden was a big step up in growability. The region is known for its deep, dark Mollisol soil type that's a gift for both farmers and gardeners and I could grow many more types of plants there than I could at the lake cabin. I still had to experiment to find out which plants could straddle the intense extremes of hot humid summers and the week or so in the winter where the low was –16 degrees and the high was –2 degrees.

The soil in my current garden on the Cape is my favorite of all—but even it is not perfect. It's obvious to anyone who looks at a satellite image of Cape Cod that it is one of the most unusual land features on the planet. It was a peninsula formed from the swoop of a sandbar left behind by the ice sheet that moved southward over the Gulf of Maine millions of years ago. Like other geographical rarities (Hawaii, Iceland, the San Francisco Bay Area, and Long Island), it is beautiful but also fragile and ever-changing. As the terminal moraine of a glacier, it resembles the little line of grit left behind on the floor when you sweep the broom into a dustpan. Similar to a sandbar or barrier island, it is always on the move and one day, thousands of years from now, the Cape will be nothing more than several isolated islands: a sandy Atlantis. Houses on barrier islands like the Outer Banks in North Carolina regularly fall into the ocean as erosion increases due to climate change and sea level rise. On our part of the Outer Cape, houses, beach staircases, beach parking lots, and even lighthouses are moved back from the edge with greater frequency every year.

Compared to the stifling effects of my clay pottery soil in upstate New York, I will take the porosity of sand any day. It does offer challenges, mainly lack of water retention and fertility. But amending it with compost, manure, and trucked-in soil helps considerably. Heading into my fourth year here, I am finding out that these amendments are not a onetime remedy. Some longtime gardening neighbors confirmed it. They need to replenish their beds as the microscopic organic materials migrate their way down through the silica, propelled by rainfall and gravity and a lack of moisture-retentive clay.

It's impossible to change the macro conditions of the places we garden: damp, heavy with clay, dry, sandy, or rocky. These are giant environmental factors that remain unchangeable in our short time on Earth. This is why it is crucial to understand the dynamics of our native growing medium so we can learn how best to improve it. Most importantly for gardeners, we're tasked with figuring out which plant species will thrive in our narrow band of land. Soil health is far from a given, and as a gift handed down over millennia, it requires our stewardship.

OVERLEAF, RIGHT: Kitchen and garden scraps well on their way to becoming compost.

LESSON

HOW TO KNOW YOUR SOIL

Soil texture falls roughly into these groups: chalky, clayey, loamy, peaty, sandy, and silty. Most gardens have a mixture of several types of soil in different parts of the garden. Loamy soil is considered the best for gardening because it is a balanced mixture of clay, silt, and sand.

- **Fistful test:** The simplest way to gain an understanding of your soil conditions is to take a handful, grasp it firmly, and release. Loamy soil will retain a ball shape but fall apart if touched. Clay soil will form a ball and retain a cohesive shape no matter what you do. Sandy soil will not make a ball even if moist. Silty soil will make a soft, unstable ball.
- **Jar test:** This easy method lets you see a rough representation of your soil makeup at a glance. Put a cup of soil (debris and pebbles removed) in a clear glass quart jar and fill it with water. Shake the jar to mix all the contents and leave it overnight. The soil will settle in layers: clay at the top, then silt, then sand at the bottom. The relative amount of each layer gives you a rough snapshot. Try several spots around your yard to compare.
- **Send-off test:** Store-bought home soil tests offer only a small amount of information. To get the most comprehensive results, send a sample to your county extension office. Check online for their specific guidelines, but in general you will gather twelve to twenty samples depending on the size of your yard. Scrape away any plant material and dig a core sample of about six inches' worth of soil. Combine all the samples in a clean container and mix thoroughly. Package some of the combined soil as directed and send off to the extension office. You can request tests, such as soil pH, extractable nutrients, heavy metals, percentages of organic matter, soil texture, and soluble salts, among others, which might vary regionally.

THE STONE GARDEN

As I've mentioned previously, creating a gravel garden of plants that would be happy in a layer of silvery pea gravel has been a dream of mine for decades. My obsession began early with the front yard of a woman who lived down the street from us in the West Texas town where I grew up. Contrary to all the keepers of trim green lawns on our street, Mrs. Ramsey topped her yard in gravel and dotted it with agaves and prickly pears, twisted mesquite trees, and a sequence of seasonal flowers, including California poppies and poppy anemones in spring. There's something dramatic about the spare simplicity of plants poking up, seemingly randomly, through a mulch of stone. I was drawn to the otherworldly appearance of her plantings—so much so that I felt I had to possess some of that beauty. I snuck down early one spring morning to snip all her anemones and a fair portion of her larkspurs, which I hid in our doghouse. I was quickly found out by my mom, who must've wondered what I was doing out there. She forced me to return the limp stems to Mrs. Ramsey, which I did tearfully. I remember her only as a shadowy figure in a doorway wearing cat-eyed glasses above a grim mouth.

My gravel garden dreams were also nourished by the books I read when I was a young rooftop city gardener, dreaming of an in-ground garden. The late English garden writer Beth Chatto's *The Dry Garden*, first published in 1978, is often credited with starting the dry or

We created a test plot to find out what would grow in sandy soil.

gravel gardening trend both in the UK and among the garden cognoscenti in the United States. Say her name and most avid gardeners will respond with "right plant, right place," a phrase she popularized in the 1960s. The phrase has become a horticultural cliché, though clichés become clichés because they're true. Her concept was simple—don't put plants where they don't want to grow. She was motivated by all the plants she and her husband had planted (and lost) over the years. It might seem odd that one of the seminal experts on dry gardening lived in England, but her region of East Anglia is one of the driest parts on the island, with an average of less than twenty-four inches of rainfall a year.

Chatto focused on plants from Mediterranean climates around the world where winters are cold but not frigid, and summers are hot, sunny, and dry. Not all such cool-wet-winter and dry-sunny-summer plants hail from areas around the Mediterranean Sea. They also can be found in coastal areas of South Africa, Australia, California, and parts of South America. These coastal plant communities share a common thread of resilience and toughness, whether they are in the scrubby *garigues* of southern France, Greece's *phrygana,* California's *chaparral,* the South African *fynbos,* or the *matorral* of southern Spain and South America. On the Cape, we have our own sandy coastal heathlands made up of bearberry, black huckleberry, broom crowberry, and lowbush blueberries that grow where trees were felled long ago by early colonists or cleared by fire. Though my garden is often dry in midsummer, one of its saving graces is the amount of maritime dew that forms on the plants overnight, adding vital moisture to the growing environment—just as in the Mediterranean.

In the 1990s, I read another influential book, *Derek Jarman's Garden* (1995), about the late filmmaker's seaside pebble garden on the southern coast of England. This austere, windswept setting has inspired a generation of gardeners, so we made a pilgrimage down to Dungeness recently to see it while in England on vacation. Jarman used what I call gap-planting, which, unlike what you might see in a packed perennial border, relies on the open spaces among the plants for visual effect, much like my neighbor Mrs. Ramsey did in West Texas.

But Jarman planted tough maritime species like California poppies and sea kale where she might've used cacti and wildflowers. He also artfully placed found objects such as driftwood and arranged bits of salvaged metal into sculptures, which inspired Chad to use driftwood, weathered stones, and remnants of silvered locust stumps to carve garden benches and create garden sculptures.

I've also begun seeking out plant varieties with "maritima" as their species name. Sweet alyssum (*Lobularia maritima*), the common annual that I've noticed growing wild on sandy sea bluffs in California, may look delicate, but it blithefully withstands drought, heat, wind, and even frost in my garden. Once sown, it'll pop up in various places for years. It's a cheerful little plant, never coming up in the wrong place but finding little bolt-holes for itself in the cracks between steps or on the edge of paving stones. I'm surprised how cold hardy it is, keeping its fluff of honey-scented white flowers long into December. Other maritimas I'm experimenting with include sea thrift (*Armeria maritima*), sea kale (*Crambe maritima*), and our own native beach plum (*Prunus maritima*), which grow well in pure sand and can be seen thriving in large colonies on even the most remote dunes. Carolina sea lavender (*Limonium carolinianum*), which is not a lavender at all but looks a bit like purple-flowered baby's breath, grows in the Outer Cape's salt marsh zones and I see it regularly on our walks fully submerged at high tide and surrounded by beach samphire when the salt water runs out. There is also a European variety, *Limonium latifolium*, I'm trying which I think might have showier flowers.

Long before we came to the Cape, I bought two books by the French author Olivier Filippi, *The Dry Gardening Handbook: Plants and Practices for a Changing Climate* (2008) and *Planting Design for Dry Gardens* (2016), in hopes that one day I'd have the chance to use them. Filippi, a dry gardening guru, is another expert on gardening in a Mediterranean climate. Just as I did with Chatto, I have to extrapolate from his ideas and adapt them to my garden on the Cape. For example, his principle of discouraging irrigation in summer because the moisture rots woody herbs like lavender, santolina, and thyme may not be practical when we have summer rains, though these have been happening less frequently. My main takeaway from Filippi has been, to borrow an Australian phrase, a "treat 'em mean and keep 'em keen" planting method. Choose plants that like sandy, infertile soil and a gravel top mulch. Dig a hole. Don't add any imported soil or amendments, plop in your plant, water the first year then taper off, and resist the urge to fertilize. Then, watch what happens.

I also find the work of Renate Kastner and Miguel Urquijo, two landscape designers that work primarily in Spain, endlessly inspiring. They use big cushions of lavender, teucrium, lamb's ears, and santolina to create rounded, biomorphic shapes that remind me of a Jean Arp painting. Surrounded by gravel or paths of crushed stone, I am trying to create a similar look with maritime, native, and Mediterranean perennials that will provide the structure of the garden, while a froth of annuals and biennials—poppies, orlaya, verbascums, and others—create a colorful but transitory froth between the forms.

I've been testing a similar concept for the past three years with mostly robust results. Some plants thrive, like certain catmint, lavender, santolina, sedums, and verbenas (both sand verbena and my beloved *Verbena bonariensis*), as well as alpines and showy tender perennials grown as annuals, such as arctotis, blue convolvulus, and gazanias. Others I thought might be successful, like geum, penstemon, and certain ornamental grasses, either dwindled under the heat and sun or didn't overwinter. Bearded irises do well, and I love them both for their flowers and swordlike silver-blue foliage.

Plenty of other plants from a variety of habitats enjoy our lean Outer Cape conditions and a water-retaining topping of gravel: bellflower, gaura, orlaya, poppies (especially California poppies), and prairie natives, such as blazing star. I use silver foliage to connect all these disparate plants together visually. One of my favorite "knitters" are the different types of dusty millers. Our wild version *Artemisia stelleriana* is familiar to anyone who has seen it growing in the dunes, though it is native to the eastern coast of Asia and the Aleutian Islands. A single-rooted cutting in my garden has turned into several plants that have grown into large, spreading ground covers over two years. I treasure it as a visual link to the magic that lies just beyond the hill where the Cape abuts the Atlantic, which is what a garden should be all about—a sense of place.

Woody Mediterranean herbs enjoy the gravel layer, which acts like a mulch retaining moisture and suppressing weeds. I've planted as many types of thyme as I can find: English, French, lemon, silver, variegated, and the creeping ones, such as fuzzy mother-of-thyme. They prefer the ample drainage and return every year without much care. But once we get the gravel garden fully renovated, I will add large areas of creepers in a flat patchwork of pinks and purples, which will pretty much stay evergreen through milder winters until spring. Rosemary, which hates wet feet in the winter, does well some years but can't take temperatures much below 10 degrees. I have one that's in its third year and I'm experimenting with protecting it from drying winter winds with a nest of Christmas tree boughs. Oregano goes dormant but returns well each year—I choose the culinary types as well as the ornamental ones grown mainly for their bold flowers, such as 'Herrenhausen', and others beloved by the bees. Marjoram, one of my favorite culinary herbs, thrives but seems to be more tender, so I plant new ones from seed every year. It dries well and I cook with it year-round. It tastes like summer.

Though we have planted and learned from many things in our gravel test plot, this spring we are planning to scrape the whole space and bring in a big delivery of new gravel once finalizing a design. I am envisioning winding pathways among islands of plants, using Chatto's triangular design concepts where a tall plant is flanked by a supporting case of lower-growing plants and ground-hugging mat varieties. It's a look borrowed from nature with a random/not random grouping and fairly dramatic height changes that range from a few inches to several feet. Right now, it exists only on paper.

While we wait for this next phase, we have been spending a fair amount of time weeding and trimming back the catmints, lavenders, and santolina, which have quintupled in size over three years. Backlit by the soft light of an Outer Cape sunset that gilds each plant's edge, this garden that combines hard stone surfaces with delicate flowers looks like Utopia to me. I like to think Mrs. Ramsey would approve.

LESSON

PLANNING A GRAVEL GARDEN

These waterwise gardens work well both in areas that get little rain or lots of rain. The gravel conserves soil moisture during dry spells while providing sharp drainage and absorption during downpours. During my time planning our garden, I have come across a lot of contradictory information, so I've tried to capture the most helpful tips here.

- Assess your native soil conditions. Heavy clay retains too much water. Gravel gardens require fairly free-draining or sandy soil. But the gravel will also retain a helpful bit of moisture underneath the plant like any mulch. Many plants suitable for this type of location, such as Mediterranean varieties, prefer leaner soils over compost-rich ones.

- Know the impact gravel has on the environment. Used loosely, gravel is a catchall term for all small stone. Technically, though, it is more rounded, formed naturally by the weathering action of water, whereas crushed stone is sharper-edged and machine-made in a quarry. Both gravel mining and crushed stone can cause habitat disruption and water quality issues, but crushed stone involves exponentially more processing and energy consumption to produce.

- Aim for a layer of gravel between three and four inches, some say six, depending on site conditions. Gravel depth is important. A thinner layer will allow bare earth or weeds to come through, while too thick of a layer can hinder plant performance and make walking or moving a wheelbarrow difficult.

- When choosing a gravel color, consider your local stone and evaluate the color in both a wet and dry state. Using local materials will help integrate the garden with its surroundings.

- Take into account the shape and size of the gravel, which is key for walkways. Rounded gravel can turn and slide underfoot, and

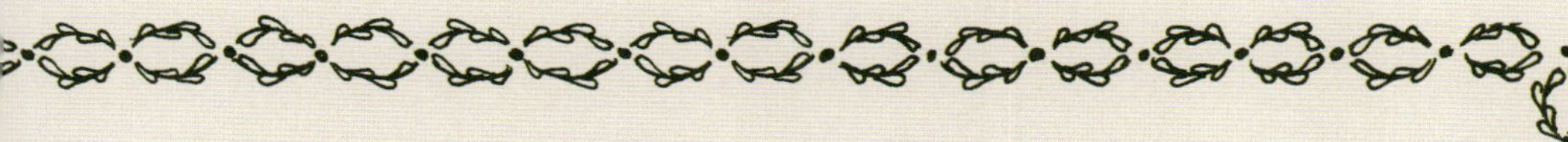

larger stones can be uncomfortable to walk on barefoot. Choose angular stones with a one-sided cleave for traffic areas, as they form a tighter bond that can support foot traffic or equipment. Fine gravel ranges from dust to ⅛ inch. Pea gravel ranges from ⅛ inch to ⅜ inch. The latter is suitable for walking but can stick in shoes and travel indoors. Smaller gravels need an edging barrier to keep them in place. Medium gravel ranges from ⅜ inch to ¾ inch and can withstand more traffic because it is heavier and doesn't move around as much. Coarse gravel, ranging from ¾ inch to 2 inches, is typically used for construction or drainage projects.

- When ordering gravel, note that the listed size in the trade reflects the filter or grate used to sort it, not necessarily the end product size. "0 to ¾" indicates a grate with ¾-inch holes, allowing material including stone dust to pass through. Specifying "¾ clean" will result in a delivery of only ¾-inch stones. "Minus" gravel products contain fine or dust-size particles, while "clean" gravel products are washed and therefore more expensive.

- Avoid landscape fabric or plastic grid systems. They are often suggested as a layer under any gravel application to suppress weeds. However, many professional gardeners know the artificial layer can make a situation worse, as weeds attach themselves to the fabric and soil health becomes compromised due to lack of aeration. I also avoid them because most products contain, or are made of, plastic, and I don't want to add that to our environment. The correct gravel depth should help stop weeds from germinating.

- Planting a gravel garden in spring or fall can work better in areas with hot, dry summers. Use smaller plants, as they require less water and grow more quickly once their roots establish. Soak each plant before placing it in a generously dug hole.

OPPOSITE AND THIS PAGE: A range of Mediterranean species and other plants thrive in the unamended, well-draining soil.

GREEN THUMBS KNOW NO GENDER

My whole life, my natural interests, the ones that have been with me since childhood and given me so much pleasure—gardening, flowers, flower-arranging, and a general fascination with beautiful things—have been questioned (at best) and ridiculed (at worst). It doesn't upset me now like it once did when a friend or random stranger would respond with "That's so gay" as an insult when I'd let my love of flowers and plants slip out in an unguarded moment. Back then I'd blush with embarrassment and swiftly change the subject. Today, I have no problem proudly sharing my love of flowers.

I do not go through my life thinking, Well, as a man, I should do this, or I won't do that because it won't seem manly enough. I'm exactly the kind of man I want to be, and I find some of the modern forms of masculinity terribly dispiriting. They seem defensive and overcompensating—like one of those giant monster Ford Ram pickups tailgating a car on the highway until it moves aside so they can roar triumphantly past. Over the past decades, gender roles have been morphing, and men are under scrutiny now more than ever about their role in our society. Some men are fine with these societal shifts, while others are not so happy about them. When did certain men get so angry? And do they really have something to be mad about or are they just hanging on to the past?

I am proudly the kid who made flower arrangements for fun—because I wanted to possess the flowers and see them close-up indoors, I think. Or maybe it was just for beauty, which I now consider to be a major way to find happiness, my raison d'être. For what is more of an antidote to the ugliest aspects of our modern world than the beauty of nature? I was also the kid who decorated the bedsheets in our house with borders of abstracted florals using washable craft paints. My parents, though both very religious and, I'm sure, full of concern about my interests, didn't discourage me from my floral pursuits. My mom commissioned me, in fact, to do my sheet décor as wedding shower gifts for fellow church members. I can only imagine the young bride-to-be's polite expression of amusement when she realized who the young floral painter was. My dad encouraged my artwork and bought me books about the Impressionists. They fostered my talents and interests in ways that were invisible to me then, but deeply touching and meaningful now. A child shouldn't have to hide their light under a bushel (to borrow the words from a Sunday school song); it might start to smolder.

The long-standing historical gender roles in horticulture are deep and stubborn. Just the word "horticulture" may seem to some traditionally minded folks to be more masculine than "gardening" because it implies a scientific pursuit that goes beyond an aesthetic affectation, a gainful profession instead of an idle hobby. For the most part, men had the roles of professional gardeners until the latter part of the twentieth century. They handled the tools, the maintenance, the hybridizing, the grafting, growing vegetables, and all the "hard" skills. Utility (male). Aesthetics (female). That simplistic narrative disregards the work of pioneering women in the field such as landscape architects Beatrix Farrand and Ellen Biddle Shipman; botanist/plant collectors like Jane Colden, Ynes Mexia, Marianne North, and Lester Rowntree; horticulturalists such as Beatrix Havergal and her life partner Avice Sanders, who founded one of the first horticultural schools for women; environmentalist Lady Bird Johnson; agricultural and civil rights activist Fannie Lou Hamer; and botanical folklorist Waheenee (also known as Buffalo Bird Woman), who taught and passed down Hidatsa agricultural techniques in nineteenth-century North Dakota—all of these women made significant contributions to our body of knowledge. And the list could go on.

When I gardened with my father as a kid (though he would call it "yard work"), we grew vegetables and flowers, but the flowers were ostensibly there to impress the neighbors or to please my mom. "Take those to your mother," he'd say as if she were the only one in the house who would appreciate them. As if beauty for its own sake were somehow a waste unless the recipient, my mom or sister, could appreciate them. It's true: My brothers would've been baffled if I'd handed them a bouquet. I protest this. Flowers are for everyone, and it drives me crazy that someone would have to ask a florist to send a "masculine" arrangement to a man in the hospital—what is that? Greenery, grasses, and pods? Are ferns feminine or masculine? What a ridiculous quandary. And in fact, botanically speaking, they can be either. If anything, flowers bloom in all sorts of forms: monoecious (male and female flowers on the same plant), dioecious (male and female flowers on separate plants), and hermaphroditic (flowers that contain both male and female parts). I've wondered why flowers are thought of as feminine. Is it because they were considered passive and stationary, waiting for the active pollinator to stop by? Seems hopelessly out of date.

The best kind of masculinity is not defensive. It isn't trying to prove anything. It listens instead of issuing orders. It creates space for others to take the center and lead. It supports behind the scenes as much as it leads from the front. It questions in order to understand rather than to undermine. It isn't afraid of progress and change. My dad, an ex–football coach who first showed me how to garden, was a great example of that. And all the while, women have expanded their roles in gardening, horticulture, landscape design, building, and science to such a degree that the professional gender lines have become welcomingly fuzzy.

As I age, I care less and less what people think. I know who I am and what I love. My role is to make the world more beautiful, if only on my small plot of land. Masculinity, like the world of plants, has an infinite range, just as femininity does. I don't spend much time contemplating or defending what my role is in any of it. I merely do what brings me joy.

Chad and me outside our first house, a lake cabin in upstate New York.

I'D RATHER BE WEEDING

I was reading an old garden book from the 1920s the other night before turning in. Quite rightly titled *The Gardener's Bed-Book,* it's a collection of pithy, clever thoughts, stories, and musings, short enough that if you fall asleep while reading them, it won't be hard to catch up where you left off. It was written by Richardson Wright who, for more than thirty-five years, was the editor in chief of my alma mater, *House & Garden* (where I was a garden editor for ten years). He wrote around forty books, many of them opinionated titles about gardening. In his bed-book, he includes a short piece on domesticalities or "observations on the everyday happenings of the household that brought a sense of well-being." He asks friends at a party for their preferred domesticalities. The responses include peeling off old wallpaper, which he describes as "having the persistent attraction of a dish of salted nuts," and "the finality of hanging up a dish towel." I enjoy that satisfying act myself after a successful dinner party.

My answer for outside the house is weeding. I don't always feel like doing it, and usually by mid-June, crafty, invasive plants, such as spotted spurge and pigroot, are getting away from me in the flower beds, driveway, and pavement cracks. When I do feel like weeding, which *does* sometimes happen, I really like to bear down. Because it's fairly mindless and repetitive work, it becomes a time when my mind can wander at will. I just select a target area (and there are plenty to choose from), sit on the grass or the back bluestone terrace, and make my way from one end to the other, pulling up unwanted plants. Like peeling wallpaper, it's a low-in-skill task with visible results.

There are best practices with weeding. These plants have evolved to be tenacious and stubborn, with varying strategies making their extraction difficult. What makes a weed a weed is subjective. I have a friend who loves the look of pokeweed with its tall, arching branches and jet-black berries that dangle like jewelry. I hate it, because the taproot is so long and tenacious and hard to extract. One plant could create hundreds of progenies if it's allowed to make fruit, which the birds eat and disseminate. Most gardeners define weeds as plants that just happen to be in the wrong place. There's another layer, though. Most weeds are highly skilled at replicating themselves. Some are good at seed dispersal (by floating through the air, being pooped out by birds, or by sticking to clothes or fur), or they have roots that could survive being buried under concrete, like Japanese knotweed, a noxiously invasive plant in a league of its own. I never resort to harmful or toxic chemicals to get rid of them; rather, I prefer to pull them out by hand or with any of my mini-arsenal of weeding tools. I have resorted to horticultural strength vinegar (20 percent acetic acid) to douse a small patch of poison ivy that crept in from the woods. Though natural, this vinegar is so highly acidic that you have to wear protective clothing, especially on your skin and eyes, to use it.

I realized last year that I had never bothered to learn the names of the weeds I commonly encounter. Though they were a constant irritant, I didn't need to waste brain space on them. Or so I thought. But knowledge is power. So I went about trying to learn more about my weeds, what they like and, more importantly, what they dislike so I can gain the upper hand. I know weeds in the garden can be a sign of a nutrition imbalance that needs to be rectified, and I'm working on that for the future. For now, I need to keep ahead of the invasives that threaten to crowd out the plants I want to thrive. Here is my targeted list of the biggest offenders:

Bittersweet nightshade *(Solanum dulcamara)* I find this stiff, lanky Eurasian vine kind of pretty with its purple nightshade flowers that resemble its close relatives—tomatoes, eggplants, potatoes, and peppers. However, it's an aggressive spreader so it must go. The flowers are followed by bright red berries, which, though tasty to birds, are toxic to us. Removal method: Give it a hearty double-fisted yank (with gloves for toxicity's sake) that will reveal an extensive system of runner roots.

Cleavers *(Galium aparine)* Also known as stickywilly, grip grass, and catchweed bedstraw, this plant is an advantageous climber that can rapidly scramble up a hedge with its Velcro-like leaves and stems, growing up to six feet when your back is turned. Cleavers may look spindly, but they have a hidden superpower—their extremely annoying seeds will attach themselves readily to clothes or animal fur. Never let the plant flower and set seed. Removal method: Grasp the stems close to the ground so you make sure you get the roots or use a long-necked tool like a Cape Cod weeder.

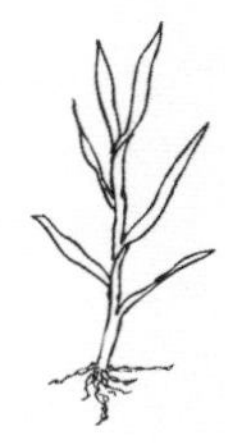

Smooth crabgrass *(Digitaria ischaemum)* Like other weedy grasses, this ground-hugging plant seems to have evolved to avoid lawn mowers and weedwackers. In summer, I find myself in a constant battle with the warm weather grass clan. Removal method: by hand in grass, or in gravel or sandy spots, use a scuffle hoe. Because it can form large clumps with tenacious roots, strike early and often when the plants are young.

Hedge bindweed *(Calystegia sepium)* Also known as devil's vine or lady's nightcap, this native morning glory relative might look dainty with its silky white trumpets, but it can be a beast due to its shallow, but extensive, root system. Removal method: Pull out by hand or with a deep weeder, trying not to leave any root scraps behind.

Horseweed *(Erigeron canadensis)* This one is super ubiquitous and super boring. It's everywhere: along the road, in the supermarket parking lot, and of course in my garden. If it's growing in a happy place, it can get very tall (around knee-height or more); in less advantageous sites, it may only be a couple of inches. As with most weeds, the key is to remove it before it makes seeds. Removal method: Pull up by the fistful. This is one of my favorite weeds to deal with because its shallow roots come up easily. Very satisfying for rage-weeding if you need that outlet.

Lamb's-quarters *(Chenopodium album)* This plant is less noxious—in fact, it's edible. A member of the amaranth/goosefoot family, it is related to quinoa and epazote and popular as a nutritious foraged green that can be prepared like spinach. Any gardener will recognize the soft gray-green leaves, which at maturity appear dusted with silver. It's very easy to pull, but please do so before it sets seed as it is extremely promiscuous. Removal method: Give an effortless tug.

Mugwort *(Artemisia vulgaris)* Also known as wild wormwood, this silvery-green plant seems to be everywhere due to its tenacious root system. Pull up one and you'll likely find several other clumps attached to the same shallow root system. Mugwort has many historical herbal uses, but in your garden, it tends to prefer the edges of beds or disturbed areas. It is so tenacious, a botanical garden I visited recently was trying steam mats as an advanced solution to get rid of it in their meadow. This is an expensive removal method that requires large equipment, so not for the home gardener. That they would go to such lengths, though, shows the serious tenacity of this weed. Removal method: Yank regularly and frequently, aiming to get as many roots as possible before it makes a larger colony.

Pigweed *(Amaranthus retroflexus)* This homely cousin of the tall, colorful garden amaranths arrives in midsummer and loves the heat. It looks like it would be easy to pull up but don't be fooled. The small radish-like pink root is tenacious and easily breaks off. Removal method: Use a long weeding tool, such as a hori hori knife or long-necked weeder, to bring up the entire root.

Pokeweed *(Phytolacca americana)* Statuesque with wide-spreading leaves and dangling purple berries, this North American native is a visual showstopper and a haven for bird life. The berries spread everywhere via our avian friends but what makes it such a challenging weed is its deep, stubborn root. Removal method: Use a shovel to dig deep enough to get the whole root.

Purple dead nettle *(Lamium purpureum)* and **henbit *(L. amplexicaule)*** I'm so fond of these two spring beauties that I barely want to refer to them as weeds. They share similar attributes, flowering in April, when very little else is blooming, providing an early food source for pollinators. Still, they spread easily and need to be kept under control. Removal method: You might allow them to bloom (but not go to seed) before pulling them up easily by hand.

Purslane *(Portulaca oleracea)* This highly nutritious garden weed is among the most commonly enjoyed by foraging cooks, along with garlic mustard and chickweed. Try it in a salad. A relative of the container-garden favorite portulaca or moss rose, it has water-bearing stems with leaves that handle drought easily in midsummer. It can often be found growing between vegetable garden rows or along pathways, looking pert on even the hottest days. Removal method: Remove easily by hand or with a hoe.

Red sorrel *(Rumex acetosella)* This is another edible weed but with tart leaves, hence the name sour grass. I inherited thick colonies of this low-growing spring weed in my front beds. It likes acidic sandy soil and tends to peter out by midsummer. It comes out fairly easily but can be exhausting because of densely growing rhizomes. Removal method: Use insistent and constant hand-pulling in spring.

Ribwort plantain *(Plantago lanceolata)* This clump-forming European weed often grows in places where the soil has been disturbed. It's distinguished from its cousin greater plantain, another common weed, by its narrow leaves and thimble-like flowers. Removal method: Grasp where the leaves meet the soil and give a strong yank or use a longneck digging tool, like a dandelion weeder, that's good for taproots.

Spotted knapweed *(Centaurea stoebe)* What a lovely sight this pink cornflower relative makes along our Outer Cape roadsides in mid-to-late summer. However, for botanists it is considered a noxious and invasive European weed. It first came to North America in a shipment of agricultural seed in the 1890s—now this biennial is everywhere. Removal method: Use a deep weeder to get the taproot.

Spotted spurge *(Euphorbia maculata)* This low-profile driveway denizen is a heat lover that will exploit every crack in your pavers or paved surfaces. It forms wide flat fans of silver-blue leaves and succulent pink stems that contain a milky sap (which, like other members of the *Euphorbia* genus, can be irritating to the skin). Its preference for dry soils gives it the apt name sandmat. Removal method: Use a paving weeder that can get into tiny cracks. In sandy or gravel areas, use a hoe.

Yellow wood sorrel *(Oxalis stricta)* Like the red sorrel, this is another edible plant nicknamed sour grass; this clover-like plant is ubiquitous as a garden weed but is easy to remove. Its pale yellow flowers bloom in midsummer. The problem is keeping up with its rampant spread, at some times of the year a daily chore. Removal method: Pull out easily by hand.

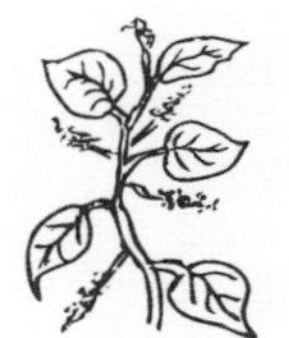

Japanese knotweed *(Reynoutria japonica)* Chad calls this The Scourge, and I saved it for last because it is in a class all its own. First imported to the States as an ornamental garden plant in the late 1800s—big mistake—it was viewed as a dangerously invasive weed by the 1930s. It's a nightmare of a plant that can grow to thirteen feet tall and turn vast areas of your yard into a bamboo-like forest. Tell people you have knotweed and, after reacting with a look of horror, they will offer a remedy that they readily admit might not work. I've heard of everything from rent-a-goat to smothering it with thick oilcloth tarps. I heard from a friend recently who is trying the latter method and hopes it will make a difference—though she said *it could take five years to accomplish.* The young spring shoots are edible if prepared like asparagus. Removal method: See methods above and try not to give up. You might need a support group. Any piece of root left in the ground will resprout.

***

Though these plants can be a constant annoyance, they are only doing what they do best—being weedy. They are programmed to survive. Just like our dog Pokey who was programmed to jump up and eat an entire Christmas panettone off the kitchen counter when our backs were turned. But I wasn't happy about that either.

THE WAYS OF WATER

If you bring up the topic of permeability in conversation, you most likely will get a blank stare. It sounds abstract and theoretical. But ask someone if they are aware that what they put down their sinks and toilets will become some version of their drinking water later and . . . now you have their attention.

I used to think of my garden as my garden only, and what I did in it was my business and no one else's. But our gardens exist in a natural society with all the geological systems that surround them. Their hydrology, the branch of science that studies how water comes into and moves out of a landscape, is one of the most important things to consider when you create and maintain a garden. My first garden, on a Chelsea rooftop, was an ecologically fragile space, but I had no concept of that back then. For the fourteen years we rented there, the many gallons of water I put into my pots and containers, all the blue-powdered Miracle-Gro I used in those days, went right down the drain, then into the municipal systems that treat the water, then back into the rivers, and, ultimately, to the ocean.

You may be thinking that doesn't sound too bad—at least the water is getting treated before being returned to nature. Many larger cities, particularly older ones in the Northeast, have something called a combined sewage system. In this arrangement, domestic sewage, industrial wastewater, and rainwater runoff flow to the treatment facility in the same system of pipes. However, when a storm overwhelms the system, the overflow, including sewage, spills over untreated into local bodies of water. When nutrients, such as nitrogen or phosphorous, infiltrate natural systems like streams, rivers, lakes, and the ocean, they cause toxic algae blooms of cyanobacteria, which harm animals, fish, and humans. This eutrophication, or excess of nutrients, also creates hypoxia (oxygen depletion) that can kill sea life in mass quantities. One of the largest examples of this phenomenon is the approximately 6,700-square-mile dead zone in the Gulf of Mexico. Runoff from large farms and other sources in the Upper Midwest overflows into feeder rivers, the Mississippi River, and, ultimately, the Gulf. If you garden near a pond or lake and use a lot of fertilizers on your lawn, you could be contributing to your own local dead zone of algae and hypoxia.

When I lived in Des Moines, I became aware of the water quality issues facing the agricultural heartland due to poor farming practices. My generation is the first in my family line not to farm. My dad grew up on a wheat and soybean farm in north Texas during the Dust Bowl years, which, in itself, was the result of shortsighted agricultural practices and soil health. In Iowa, I learned about the excess nitrogen that runs into the two rivers that meet in the middle of town, the Raccoon River and the Des Moines River. Both are fairly muddy most of the year and flow through town bringing excess runoff from the surrounding farms, some of them corporate or family-owned mega-farms that grow monocultures of soybeans and corn. Another significant source of nitrogen pollution is the manure discharge from the 24.6 million hogs and pigs (in 2024) raised on Iowa's industrialized farms under factory conditions. That's a count of around seven hogs and pigs for every human in Iowa. This is according to the local water utility, Des Moines Water Works, which has several large processing facilities to help screen out nitrates as they are among the main pollutants in the local water supply. With their "Think Downstream" campaign, they encourage both farmers and ordinary citizens to think about the interconnectedness between the local waterways and the community's drinking water.

I had tried to do my small part to help. I noticed how the rainwater in my backyard ran downhill during big storms and into a stream at the back of the property. This stream then flowed into the Raccoon, which, along with the Des Moines River, is the city's main source for the municipal water supply after going through extensive treatment. I had long ago stopped using synthetic fertilizers and had never used pesticides or herbicides, but I could see that the lawn maintenance crew who came by weekly to tend to my neighbors' yards, with their sprayer backpacks, had not been so enlightened.

I don't mean to call out only Des Moines. Water issues are gaining urgency in most communities around the world. Overdevelopment, aging infrastructure with storm sewers and septic tanks, climate change, drought, over-pumping of aquifers, sea level rise, and salinity pollution of freshwater sources are just a few of the issues facing the health of global water systems. When Chad and I moved to Cape Cod, my interest in hydrology became even more acute. Most visitors to the Outer Cape don't spend time thinking about the source of the fresh water they drink, but the process is rather miraculous. Whether a house is on municipal water or a well, it is pumped from several freshwater-filled reservoirs referred to as "lenses" that exist in our sandy soil. These lenses aren't classic aquifers, but they function much the same way, holding water that is then extracted for domestic use. I was fascinated to learn more. How does fresh water sit inside sand at a fairly shallow depth sixty-five miles out in the Atlantic? How did it get there, and how is it replenished? The answer is rainfall, but the water we use also drains back down to the lens, filtered as it percolates over time through sand and various substrates. Our hydrology is all connected.

> *It is the nature of stone to be satisfied. It is the nature of water to want to be somewhere else.*
>
> **—Mary Oliver, from "Gravel"**

Now I think about everything I put down my drains and into the soil of my garden because I know it is ultimately leaching, though filtered to legal standards, down into the lens. It takes effort to figure out what the best household products are. The more we learn about the dreaded PFAS (forever chemicals) and other contaminants that have been in household items for decades, the more vital it is to banish them from use in the home. Chad and I don't use bleach or heavy-duty cleansers of any sort. Instead, we clean with natural products or our own mixtures of vinegar and baking soda. In the garden, we never use pesticides or herbicide. I can live with a few nibbled leaves. We avoid synthetic soil amendments, and I even try to limit how much organic nitrogen, phosphorus, and potassium I add to the garden beds to keep these substances out of the local waterways and ocean.

Try to visualize your garden sitting on a giant kitchen sponge. Everything you put on top will eventually soak down below. Wherever you live and garden, what you put into your pipes and in your soil will eventually connect to the vast system of above- and belowground waterways that lace our landscape. My efforts are never perfect, but I suggest becoming aware of the bodies of water that exist around you and learn how your property's runoff interacts with them. It's a valuable place to start; one small drop in the bucket combined with everyone else's efforts makes a difference.

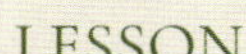

LESSON

PERMEABLE SURFACES

The goal is to keep as much, if not all, of your water on your property as possible for two reasons: to avoid wasting it and to keep nutrient-rich runoff from washing quickly into local systems. Take a walk around your yard to look at surfaces with an eye to where the water goes. Identify which materials let water soak in (like a lawn, gravel, or flower beds) and which surfaces deflect water (like asphalt driveways, concrete patios, sidewalks, or stonework set in masonry). Here are some suggestions for how to address water flow on your property.

- Add gaps of gravel or grass between paving stones for new paths, sidewalks, or a patio to allow water to soak through. If your hardscaping is preexisting, consider installing gravel or grass strips in or around impermeable pavers to catch water. I avoid plastic permeable paver grids because the materials degrade in the ground over time and add more microplastics to the ecosystem.
- Watch where your water flows the next time you have a big storm. Adding a swale, a low hollow between two mounds (also known as berms), can catch water before it runs off your property into a gutter or stream. These swales can be planted with moisture-loving bog plants in wet environments or in dry areas, constructed similarly to desert arroyos with stones and suitable plants. The swale should trap the water for long enough so that it can percolate into the soil.
- Direct runoff from rain gutters away from house foundations to beds or swales, where it can soak into the ground without running into the street.
- Reduce hardscaping in your garden, especially in areas where it's not required, and add more plantable areas that will absorb stormwater effectively.

Cape Cod's freshwater kettle ponds are a precious resource left by the glacier that created the sandy peninsula millennia ago. Their water quality is under threat from both development and climate change.

OPPOSITE: Fragrant swamp azaleas grow along the edges of a nearby pond.

WALLFLOWERS

Vivid sprays of glads at a funeral. Carnations and baby's breath wrapped in plastic printed to look like lace. Ubiquitous grocery store mums. Among certain gardeners, these flowers have been off the grow list for decades. Too pedestrian. Too garish. Or maybe just too shy and awkward to be invited to the dance.

I've noticed that some gardeners can have negative reactions to subjecting innocent plants to the whimsies of fashion, fads, and trends. Maybe such practices feel to them like unnecessarily harsh and judgy critiques about something as pure and natural as a plant. But I feel that gardening trends are meaningful, because we humans are social creatures who like to keep track of what everyone else is doing. Novel tastes and ideas also bring the attention of plant hybridizers and marketers, who give us new, and sometimes previously overlooked, plants to try. Unlike the latest thing in fashion or music that can go viral in a matter of hours, horticultural trends tend to arrive and decline, ebb and flow much more slowly—as in decades. There are definitely bandwagons that people hop on, whether it's a specific dahlia or the use of artificial turf, the latter of which came to the fore in the 2000s as a "sustainable" alternative to lawn that ended up just contaminating the environment with more microplastics as the nylon, polypropylene, and polyethylene "grass" degraded.

As I've grown in experience, I want to break the rules more. I worry much less about making mistakes, and if I do mess something up, then I've learned something new. I have a pleasurable sense of rebellion trying to grow things I've been told that I can't (although, unfortunately, the changing climate is pushing my horticultural zone number higher, so that's also responsible for much of the successes I have had).

It is both satisfying and educational to break long-standing conventions of good and bad taste in horticulture. For decades, I read garden books and articles that subtly, or more pointedly, put down certain types of plants with words like "common," "gaudy," "vulgar," or "showy." Social media, which trades in the idea that we're perpetually doing something wrong, also reinforces the notion that certain plants can be "in" or "out." What did these poor plants ever do to deserve our scorn? After all, it's us meddling humans, not nature, that breed the most ostentatious of them.

I've become more interested in plants that, to borrow a few fashion-y French phrases, are currently "de trop" (too much), "déclassé" (low class), or "démodé" (out of fashion). I remember when dahlias, especially the brightly colored dinner plate hybrids, were considered vulgar. And then, sometime in the 1990s, a new generation of gardeners discovered what wonderfully bold, prolific plants they are. Floral designers also made dahlias cool again, arranging them in loose, dusky-toned arrangements of peach, buff, and ivory. Around the same time, social media usage took off, and dahlias' popularity skyrocketed, including hybrids deemed to be more tasteful like the soft, buff-colored 'Café Au Lait'. Now, aficionados set their alarms on the days that specialty nurseries release their new offerings, hoping to snag the latest hybrids (some of which go for fifty dollars a tuber).

I got hooked on another neglected flower, the gladiola, this past growing season after I noticed people on the Outer Cape shamelessly growing them in their cottage gardens. Especially popular is a deep royal purple variety that must have been a passalong plant shared among neighbors at some point since I see it in so many gardens. Though these South African plants are overbred, and too blowsy and top-heavy for their own good, I wondered if I could incorporate them gracefully in a garden bed. I knew it would be a challenge; after all, these were Dame Edna Everage's preferred flowers, so they aren't exactly known for being subtle. I also recognized that, like dahlias or bearded irises (another once-derided, now-fashionable genus), gladiolas come in almost too many colors—so many that discipline is required. When placing my order for a spring delivery, I opted for off colors that weren't so bright: dusky purple 'Smokey', burgundy 'Black Star', chocolate brown 'Cappuccino' in one group. Chartreuse 'Kio', gold 'The Great Queen Elizabeth', and peach 'Apricot Bubble Gum' in another. My job was to keep these two groups a bit separated in the flower beds. After a search, I did ultimately find 'Purple Flora', the dark amethyst variety that resembles what's in the neighbors' gardens. I did well with the entire range, though I'll admit that their frilly blooms tend to stick out in a flower bed like a tropical orchid in a meadow. And they definitely need sturdy staking, something I can be lazy about. Seeing them lolling about at crazy angles after a windy day doesn't make them any easier to incorporate into the garden. However, I remain undeterred and plan to order another round for next summer.

For gardeners who don't want to go quite so far over-the-top, there are gladiolas the garden press has viewed as more acceptable over the years. I first learned of the gracefully slim, deep pink Byzantine gladiolus (*Gladiolus communis* subsp. *byzantinus*) in old garden magazines and books. *Gladiolus nanus*, with its smaller flowers with graphic splotches in its throat, is another, more subtle example. I grew the equally graceful Abyssinian gladiola (*G. murielae*, formerly known as acidanthera) on my roof garden in NYC for its evening fragrance and elegant white flowers dotted with a brown throat. Growing gladiolas has opened my eyes to how truly remarkable these strange, otherworldly flowers are.

Even though the bright, sturdy chrysanthemum is much more well-behaved, it's also often the victim of horticultural snobbery. I've become a big fan of the hardier versions of these plants for a very utilitarian reason. Very few plants, other than the aster clan, give the garden full-on color so late in the season. They certainly have their purpose on the front porch, or as a season-end swap in a container, though they are frost-tender plants. I find them a bit wasteful because most of the time people just toss them after a hard freeze blackens them. To counter this disposability, I focus on the hardy or Korean chrysanthemums, such as peach 'Sheffield', pink 'Clara Curtis', and mauve 'Cambodian Queen', which are true garden perennials. Planted in spring, they will grow more loosely and integrate gracefully into a garden bed in ways that a fall-planted dome-shaped mum can never do.

As for classic bedding annuals, I've liked petunias since childhood but have mostly kept myself from buying them, even on those first tempting blue-sky spring days when the annual flats come out of the nursery greenhouses. I recall all too clearly how bedraggled and mud-spattered the large, ruffled hybrids look after a rainstorm (or one of my youthful attempts at watering them with a hose going full blast). I have avoided them for being too . . . well, I don't know exactly how to express it. Too obvious? They're colorful, sometimes fragrant, and very eager to please, covering themselves with blossoms during their long season. Why am I resisting them other than sheer snobbery?

Located in the Solanaceae or nightshade family and technically a tender perennial instead of an annual, these South American natives are related to such New World crops as tobacco, tomatoes, potatoes, and peppers, and you can see the resemblance in their flared, trumpet-shaped flowers. The garden petunia we know now is a human-made hybrid first crossed and cultivated in the early nineteenth century. Over a century of intense breeding followed as hybridizers released more and more outlandishly patterned combinations to satisfy the plant-buying public. In the 1990s, calibrachoas or million bells, a close relative of petunias, were developed for the large number of small, bell-shaped flowers they produce in an expanded color range of vivid oranges and yellows.

These smaller-flowered hybrids lured me back a bit, but I fully returned my attention to petunias last summer after writing a story for *The Provincetown Independent*, our local Outer Cape newspaper, about Blanche Lazzell, a pioneering Cubist painter and printmaker who lived in Provincetown in the early part of the twentieth century. She was famous in town for the summer garden she created at her art studio out on one of the wharves, where she let vining petunias clamber picturesquely up trellises made of fishing nets. She loved petunias more than any other plant, writing about them often in her letters and selling seed packets of her unusual varieties to tourists and art students at the tea parties she hosted at her studio. In a letter to her sister in 1937, she wrote, "Sorry your petunias aren't doing well. They must have attention. If they have plenty of light & sun they won't grow spindly & tall. Care and proper soil make flowers almost talk. Mine have expression. They express God—if given the chance."

The almost outlandish flowers of the petunia were a frequent subject for Lazzell's abstractions, perhaps because of their graphic nature. Few flowers, other than orchids, have as many rays, stripes, picotees, bars, spots, and veins as petunias. After I understood Lazzell's fascination with them, I decided to do a group of pots, planted with the most graphically quirky petunias I could find. The result was fun to look at, but not much of a success. Maybe I didn't get the garish color combinations quite right. Or at least that's what the raised eyebrows of my husband and some of our judgier guests seemed to say. If we are being tasteful, I think the most elegant varieties are the solid-colored black petunias, such as 'Black Cat' or 'Starlet Velvet'. Other black hybrids like 'Midnight Gold' and 'Phantom' combine dark tones with edges or rays of pale yellow. There are several grandifloras, such as the Czech heirloom 'Greetings From Jaroměře' and the Pirouette, Superbissima, and Spellbound series, which are so intensely frilly that they look more like big blowsy poppies than petunias. My next plan is to grow a more disciplined palette of petunias from seed, but I still want it to be graphically arresting.

Carnations have also received low marks from some gardeners and floral arrangers in the recent past for their perceived vulgarity. Like mums, they are viewed as cheap grocery store flowers, perhaps because they are so long-lasting and durable (which should be a plus!). The long-stemmed florist carnations, called perpetual flowering carnations, are readily found at the corner store or supermarket and grow best in the controlled conditions of a greenhouse. Nearly scentless, they are a nineteenth-century cross between *Dianthus caryophyllus* and *D. chinensis.* Another fragrant old variety, the Malmaison carnations, also require a greenhouse because they don't do well with either winter cold or summer rainstorms. Over the past several years, arrangers like Ariella Chezar and growers like Erin Benzakein at Floret have been standing up for carnations. Erin is growing her own fragrant, long-stemmed versions from seed with successful results even out in her growing fields. Like me, she must not like seeing a flower needlessly suffer from discrimination for being out of style.

Both the perpetual flowering and Malmaison carnations are very different from the type of dianthus carnations that fit more easily in the garden. Actually, many gardeners refer to this group of plants not as "carnations," but as "dianthus" or "pinks," not because of their color but because of their edges, which are pinked (like fabric cut with pinking shears). The zigzag edge gave us the color name, not the other way around. I prefer to grow the perennial or cottage pinks (*D. plumarius*) with their clumping blue-gray foliage and graphically edged, splotched petals, such as 'Horatio', 'Mountain Frost Ruby Glitter', 'Plum Glory', and 'Stargazer'. I also appreciate dianthus with odd, frilly petals like 'Greystone', 'Itsaul White', 'Bath's Pink', and the extraterrestrial-looking fringed pink (*D. superbus*). These are all short-lived perennials and will fade out after a few years. The biennial sweet William (*D. barbatus*) has a clustered flower form and an even more intense clove scent. The unusual name of sweet William may derive from the French word for carnation or eye, *oeillet*, which sounds a little bit like "William." I am going to try growing some of these in the long border, focusing on darker colors like 'Sooty' and 'Hollandia Purple Crown'. Cheddar pinks (*D. gratianopolitanus*) and maiden pinks (*D. deltoides*) are two other popular dianthus that form ground-covering mats of fuchsia in early summer.

Wallflowers (most often biennial hybrids of *Erysimum cheiri*) are frequently mentioned in British garden media and some very old gardening books. They are not as commonly known here as they once were. Their delicately breeze-surfing, violet-like scent is the primary reason to grow them, but a warm color range is helpful too, especially with their brown and russet tones. I'm also intrigued by other historic fragrant plants such as sweet sultan (*Amberboa moschata*) and stock (*Matthiola incana*), the clove-scented gillyflowers of the Tudor period. Japanese hybridizers have taken to these old stock flowers, breeding more diverse ranges of color, such as 'Vintage Brown', pale yellow 'Ki No Mai', shell pink 'Sakura No Uta', and reddish-purple 'Murasaki No Uta'.

Just as I tend to leap to a flower's defense when others turn their noses up at it, I also take on a similar attitude about color—there are no bad colors, nor bad garden plants (excluding those that are invasive, like the odious Japanese knotweed). They just need proper companions or context. I don't usually plant the classic school bus yellow rudbeckia, partly because it's used so much, but also because it is such a strong color. However, I've seen it in naturalistic gardens where, when combined with similarly warm tones, it can really sing. If I had more room, I'd give myself the challenge to experiment with such a flower bed. Maybe I could rescue the classic black-eyed Susan (*Rudbeckia* 'Goldsturm') from the unwarranted penalty of my own prejudices. Till then, I'll be happy to admire it elsewhere (he said with a sniff).

Long banished to funeral parlors, gladiolas are making a comeback with more subtle shades such as 'Indian Summer'.

OPPOSITE AND THIS PAGE: My list of neglected varieties includes wallflowers, gladiolas, petunias, and chrysanthemums.

MY LIFE IN HOUSEPLANTS

My gardening roots stretch back to the 1970s, one of the original boom times for indoor plants. My mom went in big for the trend: macrame plant hangers, books about talking or singing to your plants, terrariums, growing avocados from pits held over a jar of water with toothpicks, filling a window with so many plants that you could barely see outside. Looking back, I'm not sure why she took to it so fully—she was a busy parent of four kids. But she made time for her hobby, and I was happy to tag along as her little helper from a young age. If you've ever shopped for a houseplant, the same selection seems to show up again and again. The reason is simple; these plants thrive in, or at least tolerate, conditions that are comfortable for humans. Before such nineteenth-century technological advances as radiators, growing plants inside was not common. Once the domestic spaces of the growing middle class were able to provide more consistently warm temperatures, a halcyon era of indoor gardening began. The Victorian period with its parlor ferneries and window displays was followed by decades where houseplants were used more sparingly and more as sculptural accents: a cast-iron plant as an accent on an Edwardian plant stand, or a graphic-leaved monstera as a piece of indoor sculpture in an art deco interior, or a spiky row of snake plants in a 1950s office lobby.

Two uncommon members of the large snakeplant family. Once *Sansevieria*, these rugged plants have been reclassified in the *Dracaena* genus.

***

In the 1970s, almost a century after the Victorian era, a second indoor gardening renaissance occurred. Houseplants became a hippie fashion statement. After another short break, indoor gardening as a signifier of coolness returned again with the hipster culture of the 2000s and 2010s. Picture all the little shops in trendy neighborhoods selling graphic shelves of succulents and pots with seventies-inspired graphics. I'm happy to say that houseplants are worth growing whether they are in or out of fashion. There is no denying the mental health benefits of having growing things around a house or apartment, especially during trying times like the COVID lockdowns. Maybe people like my mother also found solace in growing them during the turbulent social change of the late 1960s and early 1970s.

As a conservative, churchgoing, traditionalist Texan, my mom was far from a hippie. Though nationwide the Earth Day/Whole Earth Catalog counterculture was undeniably connected to indoor gardening, the phenomenon crossed ideological lines. Just look at an interior design book from those days—the rooms are filled to the eaves with plants. Jungles of ferns surrounded by spa bathtubs, vines of pothos dangling from ceilings, and air plants perched in wall displays. Houseplants were a frequent topic on talk shows and in newspapers and magazines at the time. The 1973 book *The Secret Life of Plants* by Peter Tompkins and Christopher Bird was a bestseller and the inspiration for a 1978 film of the same title with a soundtrack by Stevie Wonder. The book promoted the idea that plants are sentient beings that respond to us (beyond merely the life-giving actions of feeding and watering them, of course). At the age of eight or so, I asked my mom if we should be talking to our plants and playing music for them. She said she didn't know but it couldn't hurt. Our house was filled with music anyway. At one point, our giant console hi-fi was surrounded by a supporting orchestra of plants. I hoped they enjoyed the swelling symphonic strings from my mom's collection of Andy Williams, Mantovani, and Ferrante & Teicher records more than I did.

As I helped my mom, I peppered her with questions about the

different names of the plants and their care. Our houseplant collection was pretty standard for the time: a large dieffenbachia, scheffleras, a snake plant, a big Norfolk Island pine, a dracaena, a Chinese evergreen, spider plants, and a philodendron or two. We had so many plants my parents ended up adding a sunroom on the back of the house to accommodate my mother's growing collection. I paid close attention, learning all the names and reading Dr. D. G. Hessayon's classic *Be Your Own House Plant Expert* at the kitchen table. For years, she had two giant Boston ferns flanking our front picture window, which hung from macrame holders made from thick burnt-orange yarn decorated with wooden beads. My mom had read that ferns like tannins, so we watered them with tepid brewed tea to make their soil more acidic. Indeed, they grew luxuriously. One of my regular tasks was to help her water the hanging plants by bringing over a step stool from which we'd attach a plastic basin hung via metal hooks under the pots. The excess water streamed into the basin as we progressed from plant to plant, emptying it into the sink as it filled.

Every Mother's Day, my dad and I would go to our local nursery where I'd buy my mom an African violet. I repeated this gift for years. She displayed her collection on a brass étagère in the living room, a formal space no one ever went into except to play the piano or receive visitors, like teachers or people from church. She taught me how to feed the African violets and how to keep water off the leaves by watering them in pebble-filled trays underneath. When my mother passed away unexpectedly a quarter century later, I was touched to see the same African violets, shielded from the West Texas sun by the same sheer curtain. Their purple/mauve/pink/blue blossoms, with a hint of sparkle that gesneriads can have, looked perfectly healthy. I like to imagine that she had tended them just the day before. I took some of them back to New York City with me, but they didn't like their new home and expired. Mom had a gift for houseplants.

Like many kids during the seventies, I went through a big terrarium stage. I had several going at any given time in which I tried to create miniature worlds with rocks, moss, knickknacks from the house, or sometimes a small mirror to represent a lake. Most terrariums, mine included, look their best during the first several months before they either become overgrown, or funky from being sealed up for too long. My favorite terrarium plant from that period was called a purple passion plant (*Gynura aurantiaca*), a trailing vine from Southeast Asia that's covered in a coat of suede-like, violet hairs. I recently bought one for nostalgia's sake. As an adult, I've made several terrarium-type plantings over the years. But I prefer to do them inside containers with open tops or as dish gardens since they are easier to keep looking their best without getting mucky. The key is to select plants that like the same growing conditions, as you would in an outdoor setting. For example, cacti can be grown with succulents but never mixed with tropical rainforest species.

I didn't pay much attention to houseplants through high school and college. But by the time we rented our first apartment in New York City, I was ready to start again, though it wasn't easy to take care of indoor plants in a small studio with electric heating. Many houseplants evolved to live in tropical and subtropical forests, so they prefer a slightly cooler, more humid environment to our energy efficient homes, which are warmer and drier. Once we moved to a larger apartment with an outdoor space in the same building, I tried bringing some of my non-hardy container plants indoors for the winter with varying degrees of failure. My citrus loved my rooftop space but did not survive indoors over the winter due to the dryness and hard-to-deal-with pests like scale. Sidenote: I hate scale more than any other pest. These disgusting little insects are difficult to eliminate because they cover themselves with a waxy dome-like substance for protection. They've been around since the Jurassic period, at least, so I don't think they're going anywhere. Not only do they disfigure and kill a plant, but they also secrete honeydew. It covers everything in their vicinity, including the floor, with a sticky film that catches dust and becomes a cleaning nightmare. I don't use toxic pesticides, so I washed my plants in the shower whenever there was an outbreak. It is difficult to rid yourself of scale once you have it. Sometimes you just have to say goodbye to your plant before it infects all its neighbors—and keep a hawk's eye on them because it spreads so fast.

I tried overwintering other outdoor plants like rosemary, lavender, and other tender woody herbs in the apartment as well. But these Mediterranean natives are generally not suitable as houseplants. Even when I kept up with their watering throughout the winter, by February they looked so dried out and spent, I'd have to throw them away. It's not so much how often you water or feed them that makes the difference (most people overdo both), but the humidity levels in your home. Though many people swear by it, misting plants with a spray bottle has not been shown to be effective in creating a humid atmosphere for most houseplants. It can also cause fungal diseases. However, my husband has decided that some houseplants like misting (ferns, aloes, calatheas) and others don't (begonias). Because they all seem to be flourishing, I leave it to him.

As I moved from place to place, I've taken a more pared back approach to houseplants. Perhaps I have finally reached a state of houseplant maturity. I want fewer indoor plants to deal with, both in terms of regular maintenance but also to make being away on vacation easier. I give them tough love, watering only when I know they're dry to avoid root rot or fungi. I don't overfeed them, generally just once in the spring. If a plant starts to look puny, I will give it a spa day in the shower or sink, making sure it's deeply watered and its leaves are rinsed of dust and insects. If a plant doesn't recover, or if its pest problem is too severe (insects can sometimes come in on new plants from a nursery), then I chuck it. I know some optimistic and generous people enjoy nursing sick plants back to health, but not me. Now that I have a little more propagation room, my goal is to try to take cuttings of any ailing plants so I can start over fresh. Houseplants have always been a big part of my life, but I want to live with them as accessories, not the main event.

LESSON

HOUSEPLANT SURVIVORS

Through my decades-long houseplant journey, I've settled on a tried-and-true group of plants, some of which I've had for twenty years or more.

Norfolk Island pine *(Araucaria heterophylla)* We bought this Southern Hemisphere conifer as a small terrarium plant about twenty-five years ago. It's odd that this little tree, which is in houseplant lovers' homes all over the world, is native to only one small island in the South Pacific where its numbers are now considered vulnerably low. Our tree has moved with us through all of our apartments and houses. Its height depends on the size of the container due to root restriction. For a long time, it grew in a tall but narrow ceramic pot that kept it about two feet tall but, after crashing off a window ledge a few years ago and being replanted into a larger pot, it has shot up to five feet. This plant is indestructible. I have never found a pest on it. Seemingly, the only thing that might finally do it in would be if I overwatered it and gave it root rot.

Allspice *(Pimenta dioica)* I purchased this fragrant cooking herb as a small treelet from Logee's Greenhouses in Connecticut about fifteen years ago. It isn't large enough to produce berries (the source of the ground spice), but the leaves are scented with the same cinnamon/nutmeg/clove flavor and can be used like bay leaves in cooking. Unlike bay, though, allspice is happy indoors. In its native habitat in the forests of the Caribbean and Central America, a tree can grow to forty feet tall, but in its current eight-inch pot, it has done well with minimal care and grown to about eighteen inches high. I water it only when the leaves begin to droop, and it perks back up. A few times we've left it too long while on vacation and returned to find it had dropped all its leaves. But with a good drink it has always

resprouted and fully grown back. It responds well to a light fertilizer application twice a year with new growth and shiny leaves, and it has never had any pests.

Rabbit's foot fern *(Davallia fejeensis)* We had two of these rather odd-looking plants on the bathroom windowsill in our apartment, where they seemed to love the humidity. They completely cover their pots with a web of silvery roots. They're beautiful, if a bit creepy, because the furry roots look more like tarantula legs than rabbits' feet. When they went to Chad's studio for a number of years, they also thrived in a part-sun window. We repotted one of them in a bigger pot a few years ago and it has grown considerably larger. Many houseplants need to be repotted every few years. If you're wondering whether a new container is needed, gently pull the plant loose from its vessel. You'll know it is rootbound if there are more roots than soil and those roots are encircling and winding around themselves. It may be impossible to get established houseplants out of their pots without breaking their containers. But if an older plant is ailing, it might be worth the destruction.

Narrow-leaved snake plant *(Sansevieria* 'Fernwood Mikado') is an unusual variety of the classic snake plant with spiky leaves in that it is much slenderer and recurved than those common types. I don't know of a tougher houseplant; it truly thrives on neglect. The snake clan is among the most ironclad of houseplants. Indoors, I wouldn't water them more than once a month. My snake plant lived by itself completely unwatered in an apartment in Des Moines for more than a year during the pandemic. When I finally came to rescue it, I was amazed to see that the only signs of distress were some slightly browned leaf tips. Now it lives happily in a sunroom on the Cape—a true survivor.

A grouping of houseplants with flavorful leaves: Thai lime, allspice, curry-leaf plant, and bay.

The Nature of Oaks
whale

HORTUS CONCLUSUS

Sometimes I wonder if I'm walling myself up in my own little paradise. The concept of the garden as a refuge is well established. Derived from Old French and early Germanic terms relating to "yard" and "enclosure," the word "garden" denotes a place of separation. It is a space for keeping some things or people in, while keeping other things or people out. Historically, gardens are characterized by their vertical boundaries—fences or walls that provide both security and aesthetic value. These barriers not only protect, but they create a visual stage for what grows inside. Humans love to create boundaries. The biblical Garden of Eden was a space apart, predated by concepts of an enclosed paradise presented in older Sumerian texts. The word "paradise" itself has ancient Proto-Iranian and Old Persian roots meaning an "enclosure." Eden was a restricted space that you could be kicked out of if you ate the wrong fruit off the wrong tree. You were once inside but, now that you've violated the rules, you're outside.

The contrast between cultivated gardens and the wilderness is the basic force of garden design. The most naturalistic design seeks to control nature, even if we are trying to celebrate it by mimicking its natural elements and processes. True harmony with nature is rare. It always has the upper hand, but we can be stubborn as we try to

A fifteenth-century French manuscript of the poem "Roman de la Rose" shows the sense of enclosure in a Medieval walled garden.

control our little plot of land. Working against natural systems and demanding the perfection of zero pests, weeds, and so on only leads to stress. Accepting some disorder, maybe even a little chaos, into your garden makes it a much more peaceful experience.

When I feel overwhelmed by it all, I retreat into my garden, leave my phone in the house, and sink my hands into the earth so that I can connect with all the non-human life around me. The concept of a *hortus conclusus,* the Latin term for a walled or enclosed garden, dates back centuries but is associated with the medieval period in European art and depictions of the Virgin Mary sequestered from the world, yet miraculously the mother of Jesus. It also brings to mind the seclusion of the monks of that period and their vows to separate from the ungodly ways of the greater world. Sometimes sealing oneself off during times of trouble feels like the only thing to do. But I'm too much of a humanist to do that. I could never shut the door on society and say, "Okay, hope y'all figure it out." We all need a place to retreat to, to heal, and to reinvigorate ourselves, but there is a balance to achieve, and that's always a challenge to figure out.

Is my garden, this place I retreat to, a false refuge? On the darkest news days, it's okay to retreat into the flower bed as an act of self-preservation. It's a safe space but also a place to rebuild one's strength before heading back out into society. I think we can celebrate the protection our gardens offer without turning into hermits.

Sociologists discuss the concept of "third places," those spaces we gather with strangers as part of a selective community. If "first places" are our homes and "second places" are our work, "third places" consist of coffee shops, town squares, gyms, community centers, temples, and churches where we can gather and find kinship through proximity. A 2024 Harvard survey identified that nearly a quarter of Americans regularly feel lonely, with 73 percent identifying technology as a contributing cause for their loneliness. Somewhat surprisingly, younger members of the study reported higher rates of loneliness, with 29 percent among those in the 30–44 age group, and 24 percent in the 18–29 age group. Only 10 percent of those over the age of 65 reported the same feelings. One of the main side effects of technology is self-isolation, primarily through the attention-absorbing effects of social media or gaming.

When I watch other people in public places, it is rare to see someone just sitting and looking at who and what is around them. Gardening, especially in a group setting like a community garden, can become a valuable third place. It also knits a gardener with their neighbors and even their local nursery owners to trade plants or share advice or weather reports. Gardening may be something of a solitary pursuit in the actions of planting and weeding, but once you're a gardener, you're a member of a global community of like-minded enthusiasts.

More than ever during these times, I am trying to strike a balance between sticking my head in the sand and overconsuming information—especially news. Putting conscious limits on my social media time allows many more hours in the day for analog pursuits, whether they're experienced at a third place or by gardening in my own backyard. I hope that everyone can have the opportunity to cultivate their own sane space, whether it's a windowsill garden, a condo backyard, a farm, a community garden plot, or a public greenspace—a walk in Central Park has soothed me on many stressful days. These separated spaces are where we engage with Nature with a capital "N" one-on-one. Nature has always owned our gardens. We are just the maintenance crew. If we do it right, Nature recognizes what we are doing and becomes a collaborator. That's when the real magic happens. You see an insect, bird, or snake you've never seen before. You admire a flower you forgot you planted the previous fall and realize you didn't sow it—it's a wildflower. You notice the tree you planted three years ago suddenly and mysteriously shoots up in height. These are the real connections, not just the aesthetics. They remind us that when all the toil and spin of human history ceases to exist, the Earth will continue on, repairing itself leaf by leaf, drop by drop, wing by wing. Ad infinitum.

An elegant sequence of garden rooms at Hollister House in Washington, Connecticut.

VISITATIONS

Often the best ideas come from our own imaginations, but occasionally they arise while visiting other people's gardens. In my line of work, I've had the pleasure of seeing many inspiring gardens around the world. Reflecting on them now is like moving through time, from one hedged-in garden space to another. I am fascinated by what other homeowners might be doing that I'm not, what plants they're growing, how they're using color, and most importantly, what design concepts they're employing that I could borrow and adapt.

Hollister House Garden in Washington, Connecticut, is an example of a private garden that has greatly influenced me. The twenty-five-acre property was carved quite literally out of a hillside over the past forty-six years by George Schoellkopf and Gerald Incandela. Their terraced garden wraps around an eighteenth-century house in a classically English style, mixing formality and looseness to great effect. Massive blocks of yew separate wide borders filled with unusual shrubs, perennials, and annuals. It's a plant collector's garden with a design focus, so that it doesn't look like a random collection of rarities. Instead, pathways and steps wind through the plantings, leading up and down various levels, through gates and openings in the hedges. Like the twentieth-century English gardens, such as Great Dixter, Hidcote, and Sissinghurst, that inspired the design, the gardens at Hollister House evoke excitement and a sense of discovery with the rounding of each carefully executed corner. Color experimentation is key: red, brown, and black. White, silver, chartreuse. The level of artistry and horticulture is something I strive toward in my own garden, so when I visit, I ask a lot of questions.

Luckily, gardenmakers are by nature very generous. If a visitor admires a plant, it's customary for them to offer up a cutting or some seeds, if the timing is right. They also share sources for special plant varieties or hardscaping materials like reclaimed stone. This cross-pollination of ideas is essential to the creative life of a gardener. On a garden stroll around Hollister, George and I might compare notes on what he can grow in his heavier, more fertile soil in colder Zone 6, while I share what successes I have in my less fertile, free-draining position near the sea in Zone 7B. I'll usually snap photos of the plant combinations or design ideas and take notes on the hybrids and online plant sources he recommends. I rarely leave any garden I visit without feeling more informed and inspired.

Aside from being generous, gardenmakers can also be a little envious and a touch dissatisfied—not in a negative way, but in a constantly growing way. Gardens never stop changing, so we are always responding and adapting to them. We often want what we don't have, and then not having it makes us only long for it more. A gardener with a steep slope might wish for a level spot to make a flower border. For me, I have a relatively flat property. Walking around Hollister House Garden, with its levels and elegant transitions between the various garden spaces, makes me want to figure out how to mimic some of that topographical drama.

Even gardens in different climates than mine can inspire. I consider Lotusland in Santa Barbara, California, to be at the top of this list for style and sheer originality. Created over several decades by the eccentric and highly creative Madame Ganna Walska, the garden pushes both plant expertise and surrealism to the edge. Though I'm not able to grow giant silver agaves, aloes, and palms in New England, I can create a garden area of serene silver and blue foliage like the one she designed. I could also add decorative touches made from found objects and salvage materials like the large pieces of blue glass slag from the nearby water bottling factory that Madame Walska used to line her garden pathways. Never bound by tradition, she used abalone and giant clamshells from the South Pacific to decorate a reflective moon pool in her aloe garden. Hers is a shallow but large concrete kidney-shaped pool that she painted white to catch the moonlight. I am intrigued by the idea of a moon garden out on the Cape with some sort of low moonlight-catching water feature. And I have a ready supply of smaller, native clamshells lying around. Perhaps mine could be a smaller, shallow concrete disc, twenty-four to thirty-six inches wide, surrounded by mounds of silver leaves and white flowers that pulls the full moon down into a gravel garden on clear summer nights and makes an eye-catching garden feature when I step outside to look at the garden before bed.

When I moved to New York City decades ago, I would visit Wave Hill, a public garden in the Bronx, as often as possible to satisfy my cravings for open space and nature. I was just starting to learn about horticulture, and the horticultural practices at this garden are unparalleled. The property overlooks the Hudson River and the Palisades in New Jersey from a high perch, with little in its viewshed to let on that it's still within the city's borders. It is large at twenty-eight acres, but because it was formerly a family estate, the gardens near the main houses have a domestic scale to them. Over many visits, at various times of year, I learned a garden should interesting in every season.

In spring, bright blue glory-of-the-snow flowers blanket several large slopes and create pools of color under the collections of giant trees. In midsummer, each square of the formal quadrants of the flower garden next to the conservatory overflows with unusual combinations of flowers and, most importantly, colored foliage. In the autumn, an old sculptural staghorn sumac (that to many visitors might look like a weed tree from the roadside) has been allowed to sprawl like an overgrown bonsai with its scarlet-draped limbs resting on the ground in the middle of the Wild Garden. In winter, special attention is paid to trees and shrubs that exhibit bright winter berries, such as the rare igiri trees (*Idesia polycarpa*) with their dangling racemes of red. Winter blooms such as witch hazel (*Hamamelis*), Himalayan sweet box (*Sarcococca hookeriana* var. *humilis*), mahonia, and wintersweet (*Chimonanthus praecox*), are dotted around the property to catch you off guard, not only with their fragile blossoms in the gray landscape, but also with their unexpectedly fine fragrance.

Two more New York City gardens that have greatly influenced me are the Conservatory Garden in Central Park and the vast New York Botanical Garden in the Bronx. The former has three sections in its formal design: a circular garden, a central lawn with a fountain and wisteria pergola, and an intimate flower garden surrounding a water lily pool and hedged in by lilacs. I find the circular garden thrilling in the fall with its candy-colored assortment of hardy Korean mums. It inspired me to seek out and plant my own. Now in their third year in my garden, many of these hybrids are thriving as vivid reminders to never go quietly into winter. The flower garden was renovated and redesigned in the 1980s by two noted garden designers, Pepe Maynard and Lynden Miller. I first saw their use of unusual annuals here in the 1990s, and it was a revelation. These were not arranged as low-bedding plants of petunias, begonias, and lobelias. Instead, taller annuals, such as globe amaranth, purple angelonia, coleus, ornamental okra (*Abelmoschus manihot*), dark sweet potato vines, green-cupped tobacco (*Nicotiana langsdorffii*), and *Verbena bonariensis*, were used like perennials to create dynamic drifts of color and texture between low yew hedges. Once fairly rare, these annuals are now more available in garden centers. Every year since that visit, I've depended on easy, free-blooming plants like these to fill gaps in the gardening schedule.

The acreage of the New York Botanical Garden is much more expansive than that of the Conservatory Garden and, tucked around its rolling woodlands, is a series of more domestically scaled gardens that inspire thousands of visitors a year. The Native Plant Garden has encouraged me to appreciate the beauties that exist right under our noses in the Northeast, such as white baneberry (*Actaea pachypoda*), wild blue phlox (*Phlox divaricata*), ironweed (*Vernonia noveboracensis*), and fragrant swamp azalea (*Rhododendron viscosum*).

All these gardens are either public institutions or, in the case of Hollister House, open to visitors, but I find private examples even more relevant, because their scale is more intimate. The first time I visited my friend Susan Burke's garden in Nantucket was many years before I ever imagined I too would live by the sea and make a garden under maritime conditions. For her flower-forward property, Susan had been inspired by *An Island Garden* (1894), in which the author, Celia Thaxter, wrote about the garden she created on the Isles of Shoals, a cluster of islands off the coast of Maine. The simplicity of Thaxter's plantings—mainly classic perennials combined with roses, poppies, love-in-a-mist, larkspurs, and hollyhocks—inspired the seaside cottage style of Susan's garden.

To help her fragile plants survive just steps from the sea, Susan installed a version of a landscape design device called a ha-ha at the urging of our mutual friend George Schoellkopf. In eighteenth-century England, the concept of a ha-ha was to create a sunken barrier or pit that prevented livestock from coming from the fields into the lawn areas around a manor house. From the house, it was invisible, but once you came upon it your surprised response would be "ha-ha!" In Susan's garden, the ha-ha isn't there to keep out livestock but to provide an eight-foot-deep shelter from the wind, lined with rough stone walls and featuring a pathway along the bottom dotted with the more delicate flowers. On top of the garden walls, an array of tall, wispy plants like alliums, gaura, globe thistles, poppies, Russian sage, and sea hollies wave in the breeze next to the harbor. Many of my planting ideas at the Cape have been influenced by what Susan and her garden designer Julie Jordin have accomplished at their seaside location—a combination of careful planning that appears loose and romantic like a beach garden should be.

Our Cape Cod garden is still very much a work in progress and we're always looking for new ideas to improve it. When we show visitors around, I usually find myself making excuses for what's not done yet or isn't quite where I want it to be. The chain-link fence we haven't disposed of around the former dog run, the dead yew stumps that didn't survive being transplanted, the lid to the septic tank we haven't figured out how to conceal. Gardeners are known for their excuses to visitors, so much so that nurseries commonly sell little decorative script signs that read "You Should've Seen It Last Week." When it comes to my garden, I do my best to follow Julia Child's advice for serving a dinner you've cooked for guests—never apologize, even if it's warranted. Still, I can't help but wave away compliments with phrases like, "Oh, thank you, but it wasn't quite the color I thought it would be," or "I had no idea it would get so large." I try to remember to just say "thank you" and leave it at that.

The garden images in my head can be hard to translate to visitors. The three European hornbeam trees we planted a few years back have not grown as well as I'd like. In my mind, they stand about thirty feet tall in a row where their branches gently touch, almost like a stilt hedge that might be found in a European estate garden. The front garden of the house has a walkway to nowhere flanked by a couple of overly formal yews planted ninety or so years ago. We are gathering ideas to turn this into more of a brick terrace that matches the formal symmetry of the house, but we haven't even put pencil to paper yet to sketch it out.

Even though the garden isn't ready, I enjoy hosting visitors. When I start waving around to explain what glories await in the future, I can tell those who get it and those who don't. I don't blame the latter. I do not always adequately convey what I am visualizing so clearly in my head. Given enough time and effort and with an adequate budget, though, I know we'll get there. Having people stop by and ask me questions and offer ideas helps me move forward—eventually. A garden is never finished. For if it were, it would end. And that, for any gardener, is a fate worse than death.

The glorious visual cacophony of the chrysanthemum display at the Conservatory Garden in New York City's Central Park.

Susan Burke's garden in Nantucket is filled with delicate cottage garden flowers that thrive within a few steps of the harbor.

FAITH IN A SEED

The first time I walked outside on a March morning and scattered a handful of hardy annuals seeds on the snowy flower beds, I felt the same way I have the few times I gambled at a casino—like I was throwing money on the ground. I had no idea when, or even if, the seedlings might come up. But for the relatively cheap price of a few packets of seeds, I was ready to take the chance.

And it worked. In May and June, the payoff arrived without any help from me. The previously bare patch of soil near my front door erupted in a constellation of alyssum, clarkia, cornflowers, gilia, phacelia, sweet sultan, tidy tips, and poppies of all shades and hues. I was enchanted by a new (to me) category of plants: direct-sown hardy annual flowers. Horticulturally, the term "hardy" means the plants will germinate in, or at least not be damaged by, the cold temperatures of most winters and early springs, while "annual" refers to living only one growing season before setting seed. Another class is the half-hardy annuals, which includes cosmos, marigolds, nicotiana, and zinnias. As "half-hardy" indicates, these plants are differentiated by how they respond to cold temperatures, with half-hardy plants being more susceptible to frost and more tolerant of summer heat than hardy annuals.

Some gardeners think annuals are a waste of time and money because they must be replaced every year, instead preferring perennials, which

The aptly named 'Cupcakes Blush' cosmos.

return each year but usually bloom for only a short time. Annuals bloom their cheerful little heads off in a live-fast-die-young kind of frenzy. They're designed to procreate quickly. I've grown to love them for their ease but also because they're generally inexpensive. Seed packets range from a couple of bucks to five or six dollars for the more fashionable varieties. By growing the widest spectrum possible, I am also getting the widest range of bloom times and variety to extend the season as long as possible.

I developed my technique of scattering seeds on bare soil in Des Moines, where I cleared an overgrown flower bed in the backyard one spring day and then didn't know what I wanted to plant. I didn't know how long I would be in that house, because it was job-dependent, and I worked in the ever-shifting world of media. After pulling the weeds and adding some new soil, I decided to plant annuals because they are quick and low-commitment, and I knew if I added some larger varieties, like tithonia and cosmos, I'd have a big show by midsummer—and I did. The poppies, especially the larger flowered ones like 'Hungarian Blue' and 'Hen and Chickens', shot upward. It's not only the otherworldly flowers they produce, like intricate frilly bowls decorated with pincushions of stamens, but their foliage is fascinating to observe as well. The glaucous, jade-colored leaves unfold from the stems, each ending in a curving crook with a downward-facing bud covered in whiskers. After a rain, the surfaces of the leaves and petals repel water to form balls of quicksilver. I'm obsessed with this remarkable group of plants: from the robust breadseed poppies to the Shirleys, and in all their colors and forms, from the scarlet singles to the pastel-fringed doubles, and from the bright pompoms to the silvery ruffles of 'Amazing Grey'. These wonders possess incredible genetic variation with hues and forms that morph and switch, even within named hybrids. How can such flamboyance emerge from such a tiny dot of a seed?

Later in the summer, my tithonia plants next to the driveway became giants. Each one six or seven feet tall, with spreading stems up to four feet wide covered in bright orange daisies that attracted butterflies and hummingbirds. My cosmos grew wonderfully too—the only challenge was keeping up with the deadheading so they would bloom as long as possible—hopefully till frost. This garden was the first place I experimented with growing tender perennials as annuals as well, adding four-inch seedlings of tall, shrubby Mexican salvias that I knew would get to five feet or so by late summer and carry on till fall. Since then, I always include them to span any late-season gaps.

I am still experimenting with what will reliably grow from seed on the Outer Cape, but the evidence tells me this is a perfect place for these plants. Our winters generally aren't super cold except for the rare below-zero cold snap. Our soils are well draining. Spring normally provides plenty of rainfall, though that seems to be changing the past couple of drier years. The sea breezes are moist and gentle, unless there's a raging storm. All that's required from the gardener is to open the seed packet and scatter the seeds wherever they want the plants. Most annuals don't like competition. The seeds will usually get lost and not take hold in an established bed, so I either clear an area of plants or dump several inches of soil and compost on top of bare earth to give them the best chance for success. Keep in mind that shorter varieties like alyssum, California poppies, clarkia, and phacelia need to be sown at the front of the beds so they don't get lost among taller types. I scatter a broad ribbon of these along the front of the beds like a ruffle, and they always fill in beautifully.

Larkspurs have been one of my favorite hardy annuals since I first saw them growing in my neighbor's side yard as a child. I loved the cloud of blue they produced. And their short flowering period made them seem rare and special each spring (in Texas, larkspurs come out early because they fade in the intense summer heat). To clear up any confusion, larkspurs are annuals and their look-alike cousins, delphiniums, are perennials. Every time I tried to grow larkspurs in one of my previous gardens, they played hard to get. I attempted them in containers on my Manhattan rooftop, but they never showed. The conditions were too shady at the upstate cabin to get them to take hold. Even in Des Moines, where there was sun and relatively decent soil once I amended it, they failed to germinate. Of course, their elusiveness only intrigued me more, especially the mixed-blue hybrids and the lilac-gray 'Smokey Eyes'.

My first two Cape seasons I had trouble getting the larkspurs to germinate, but after a little research I learned that they could benefit from a process called "cold moist stratification" to break their dormancy. The process is as follows: In January, I placed the larkspur seeds in small, sealed jars with a bit of damp soil and kept them in the refrigerator for about a month, until I saw them just begin to sprout. Then I tucked the clumps of soil, tangled with what looked like little alfalfa sprouts, into a cleared patch of soil that was free of any competing weeds. It worked well, and by late June I had a robust tangle of larkspurs, which have now self-seeded all over the place, the way many hardy annuals do. Once I have them, it seems I will always have them. When they come up in the wrong place, like they did in a raised vegetable bed that had previously been for cutting flowers, I easily moved them. I found the best and less disruptive method was to lift them with a shovel in April, keeping as much soil under the seedlings as possible. This slice of seedlings can then be placed gingerly in a more suitable flower bed. By June, my front flower bed was chest high in larkspur spires.

Most direct-seeded annuals don't require such special consideration. They want the basics: water, sun, and decent soil. If I stagger my hardy annual plantings and follow them with half-hardy varieties, such as cosmos, zinnias, and balsam impatiens, in May, I'll get continuous bloom till frost. Especially with heat-loving cosmos, which come in a dazzling array of colors and forms. Once you get started, it's easy to save these seeds because they're so prolific and easy to grow. They are exceptionally bighearted and generous for their size and though their blooms might be fleeting, the visual impression they make is infinitely memorable.

OVERLEAF, LEFT (*clockwise from top left*): A collection of poppies: California poppy 'Pink Champagne', 'Amazing Grey', 'Feathered Mix', 'Lauren's Grape'.

OVERLEAF, RIGHT: Direct-sown cosmos and sweet-corn create a tall "meadow."

LESSON

SAVING SEEDS

Most annuals make a lot of seeds, so collecting them is both easy and economical. Here are some seed gathering and storage tips that will keep your harvest viable till the next growing season.

- Let the seeds fully ripen on the plant. They should look dried and usually golden or brown.
- Harvest the seeds after a few days of dry weather, if possible, but before they fall from the stems on their own. We take small paper bags and cut the seedheads over the bag to retain as many seeds as possible.
- Let the seedheads dry indoors on a piece of paper or a cookie sheet, or you can hang them in bundles. Once they are completely dry after several days, process them by removing as much of the stems as possible. Keep your various seed sources separate and make sure they are not holding any moisture or they might rot over time.
- Place the seeds in paper or glassine envelopes that are carefully labeled. Put larger amounts of seeds, cosmos, or digitalis, for instance, in glass jars with paper labels inside. Store them in a cool, dry location out of the sun. Some plants are so generous with their seeds that you'll want to give them away to gardening friends.

'Hungarian Breadseed' poppy

OPPOSITE: A tall stand of the ever-elusive larkspurs.

THE RAINBOW GODDESS

I was looking at a bearded iris the other day, watching a bee tumble its way through the folds, ripples, and petals, drunk with pollen-dusted happiness, and I thought, That's me. That bee embodies exactly how I feel about these marvelously flamboyant flowers.

I'm fascinated by their expansive color range, going from snowy white to jet black (I think among the blackest of any flower). And most of the spectrum between, except for true green or scarlet. They are named for Iris, the Greek goddess of the rainbow and a messenger between the gods and humanity, skimming back and forth on her colorful bow. I have grown these perennials in every place I've gardened, mostly with limited success. Some spots were overly shaded; in others, the soil was too heavy, but on the Cape I have finally found iris heaven.

The bearded iris (*Iris* x *germanica*)—the "beard" refers to the fuzzy bee strip on its petals—is thought to be a naturally occurring hybrid of central and southern European native irises. Over the centuries, thousands of varieties have been bred. Given the wealth of color choices available now, it has become a challenge to arrive at an intentional color palette. I was immediately drawn to the off shades: dusty, in-between colors like fawn, mahogany, mauve, olive, oyster, puce, rust, and, of course, the blackest ones I can find. The color names indicate that these are not primary colors but the kinds of blended, or even muted, colors an artist might create.

An iris sampler in shades of brown, blue, and deep purple.

I first fell in love with these moody shades several years ago when I discovered the paintings of Sir Cedric Morris (1889–1982), who bred and painted irises at Benton End, his house in Suffolk, England. He also ran an art school there with his life partner of sixty years, artist Arthur Lett-Haines (1894–1978). They taught young Lucien Freud and other students how to paint plein-air in the garden. Morris doted on misty, subtle tints, especially the buffs, grays, and browns that also obsess me. In the UK, some of his extant hybrids have become collectors' items (most with the name Benton in their titles). He favored plicatas as well, irises featuring stippling, lines, or shading on their edges. I have yet to find a mail-order source in the United States, and trust me, I've looked. Not one to be thwarted, I've tried to gather as many off colors as I can from specialist American sources online such as Schreiner's Iris Gardens. Some of my favorite oddballs include: 'Coffee Trader', khaki with sapphire centers; 'Friendly Advice', a silvery ecru; and the oddly named 'Wench', soft peach with deep eggplant falls (the part of the flower that drops downward). I complement these with black flowers, such as 'Before the Storm', 'Black Suited', or 'Cosmic Voyage', and the pale ice blues, such as 'Abiqua Falls' or 'Nestucca Rapids'.

When friends visit, I encourage them to smell the different iris blooms to see if my childhood theory that scents match their colors holds up. Invariably, like in *Willy Wonka & the Chocolate Factory,* they do. Browns smell like root beer. Yellows like lemons. Purples like grape, specifically grape candy or gum. Others smell like divinity fudge or have a perfume that can only be described as powdery. White doesn't actually smell like coconut—although it could to the easily suggestible. Comparing scents among the different iris plants is truly a transporting activity. It sends me back to my six-year-old self on Texas mornings in my neighbor's front yard where she grew dozens of them. These delicate-looking flowers like hot, arid West Texas very much.

Given the right conditions, irises are tough and low maintenance. They don't mind being transplanted; in fact, they need it once in a while. A midsummer division of larger clumps of rhizomes every five or so years will yield more flowers and stronger leaf growth. Midsummer is also the time to plant new rhizomes, and iris placement makes all the difference. In our Cape climate, where it's not too hot, iris rhizomes should be planted so they are partially exposed to the sun, orienting the fan of leaves so the root faces the light for most of the day. They prefer free-draining, sandy soil to help prevent root rot over the winter. For heavier soil, plant them in a larger hole that's been amended with grit or sand.

Irises make a big visual statement on their own in both flower and leaf and planted along a wall or fence. Or if you want to feature them in a mixed border, plant them at the very front with some space around their roots. They like to be the star, not crowded or shaded by other plants. There is a marked difference between my 'Beverly Sills', which has quadrupled in size in a gravel garden setting where she has no one around her, and my 'Edith Wolford', who spent the last two summers too near a sprinkler overwhelmed by a giant catmint. In her third year, Edith let me know that she would like to be moved by sulking and going on a bloom strike. Irises have a limited bloom time—just a few weeks—but what a grand impression they make in such a short period. For the rest of the growing season, their glaucous, sword-shaped leaves create useful vertical accents in the garden. With their large heads and spindly bodies, staking is often required. They're loud and brash and maybe even a little too much. "Well, hello! Where's the party?" said a friend when he saw my collection. Then again, if they bloomed all summer, then we might not appreciate their fleeting glory as much. As the old showbiz saying goes, "Always leave 'em wanting more." And that's exactly what irises do.

LESSON

HOW AND WHEN TO DIVIDE IRISES

Bearded irises thrive and increase if they are divided every few years to keep their rhizomes from overcrowding. This is best done in midsummer after they've flowered. Follow these steps:

- Carefully lift the plant from the ground with a spade or garden fork and shake off most of the soil. Trim the leaves to about six inches so that the plant has an easier time as it reestablishes and puts energy into its root growth.
- Untangle the roots and slice the rhizome into separate pieces with several leaves attached. Cut off and discard any soft or rotted sections of the rhizomes. Let the cut pieces dry and heal for a few days.
- Replant the irises in a sunny, well-draining position. Add a little bonemeal to a shallow hole if your soil isn't fertile. Make a small mound in the center of the hole and fan out the roots, leaving the top of the rhizome exposed to sunlight. Water well and wait for next spring's flowers to arrive.

'Beverly Sills' iris rules supreme in the gravel garden for a few weeks in May.

OPPOSITE: The unusual tan and blue coloring of 'Mocha Frappe' iris.

The intricate blooms of bearded iris merit closer appreciation indoors.

The Long Border at the horticulturally influential Great Dixter in East Sussex, England.

PARDON MY ANGLOPHILIA

I think my love of all things British started with early family trips to England. The first time was in 1977 and it made a huge impression on me coming from a town of ninety thousand in West Texas. It was the year of Queen Elizabeth II's Silver Jubilee, though we didn't realize that until we arrived in London. I remember the crowds and how hot that summer was—even for us Texans. We were horrified at their lack of air-conditioning and dismayed with British cuisine as it was in those days. On several visits we stayed at Manzi's, a tiny family-run hotel off of Leicester Square above an Italian seafood restaurant of the same name. Everything smelled vaguely of calamari, and even though as a very picky child I could barely choke down a Mrs. Paul's fish stick, I loved the experience. The wallpapered rooms were charmingly old-fashioned and foreign (to us at least), with an echo-filled tiled bathroom and a giant clawed bathtub that seemed more fit for *Downton Abbey* than the rooms above a fish restaurant. What I was most fascinated about, other than the great age of everything, were the gardens and parks. As a concept, an English garden denotes a loose, flowery planting style, something very different from the tight foundation shrubs, minimal flowers, and clipped lawns I'd grown up with. Where our yards looked respectable and a bit sterile, the English versions seemed romantic and full of humanity. What makes an English garden an English garden?

The related "cottage garden" has been used frequently in garden books and magazines over the years, often with no indication of what it means exactly. Its popularity became widespread in the early twentieth century when gardeners of higher socioeconomic classes began to idealize and mimic the small yards of working people. The idea was that a worker who was employed at a great estate garden might bring home cuttings or seeds to grow in their own plot. These gardens were viewed as honest and authentic because the overall effect was one of random beauty—disparate plants and one-offs tucked into a charming setting behind a low wall or picket fence. This story of the naïve worker's garden feels reductive and condescending today, but it's definitely a construction with deep roots in the anti-industrial Arts and Crafts movement of the period.

The main proponent of the romanticized cottage garden style was Margery Fish (1892–1969), an author and magazine columnist who created a garden in Somerset from the late 1930s into the 1960s. She and her husband bought a derelict manor house for one thousand pounds and made a garden together, often (as she reported) with a lot of humorous squabbling. Her 1956 book, *We Made a Garden,* tells the story of the power struggles between her neatnik husband, who valued tidiness and order above all, and her more tousled, flowing approach. She wanted her plants, often dainty heirlooms, to self-seed and pop up between the gaps in the flagstones or tumble out of crevices in stone walls. She recounts how, after being instructed by her husband to not put in any more plants between the pavings, she snuck out after he went to bed and chiseled gaps in the rocks to create more spots for them. To this day, when my husband tells me we don't need any more plants, I just think WWMFD? And I buy more. I recently made a pilgrimage to East Lambrook Manor, her former home that is open to the public, and found it as charmingly floriferous as I had hoped it would be. All these years later, it is still under private ownership and, by chance, I arrived on the day the new owners were taking possession with the best intentions for continuing Margery's cottage garden traditions.

What makes English gardens work so well is the idea that you can be as messy as you like—but you need to contain the chaos with geometry. Big flower borders look their best with the backing of a clipped hedge or wall. The front of garden beds can be hemmed in by a low boxwood edging. If plants such as catmint are allowed to spill onto a walkway, then that walkway should be tidy. I've heard gardeners say as long as you keep the hedges clipped and the paths swept, the rest can be a bit of a mess. This appeals to me as someone who is almost always more interested in the gesture rather than perfection.

On a recent trip to tour gardens around the southern part of England, we made a visit to the two English gardens that possess the largest fan clubs of Anglophilic gardeners: Great Dixter and Sissinghurst. Both were created in the early part of the last century, but the paths they've followed since the death of their creators have been very different. Sissinghurst is part of the National Trust, while Great Dixter is run by a private trust. Both exhibit the design combination of straight-edged hedges and topiaries mixed with billowing drifts of shrubs, perennials, and annuals that I mentioned before. Sissinghurst is gardened expertly but more tightly, with an emphasis on Vita's old roses and newer, more inventive color combinations. At Great Dixter there is a more noticeable sense of experimentation with the loose, and some would say even messy, side of the horticultural conversation that is going around in garden circles these days. Many gardeners are looking for ways to entice more wildlife and biodiversity to their properties, and Great Dixter has taken this on as a primary focus. Some of the hedged-in garden rooms are edited very loosely, allowing waving stands of cow parsley and other beautiful interlopers to weave through and around as they nearly block the narrow walkways.

The wildlife-centered aspect of modern horticulture is even more apparent at Knepp Castle in West Sussex, where the owners, Charles Burrell and Isabella Tree, have rewilded their 3,500-acre estate over the past twenty-five years, allowing the former farm fields to return to something resembling their original, pre-agricultural state. We went to see their latest self-described experiment, a Victorian walled garden that formerly housed a kitchen garden and a large croquet lawn. Several years ago, all of that was removed and a hilly landscape of gravel, sand, and debris was installed to be a biodynamic haven for pollinators and wildlife, while also pushing the limits of a no- or low-irrigation approach to maintenance. Even England is experiencing more heat and drought than it has in the past, and the plants the gardeners have chosen are very much like the ones I want to grow in my own seaside garden: tough, drought-tolerant, and elegant in their simplicity. These are not lush peonies or thirsty tropicals, but species that don't mind being between a rock and a hard place—in fact, they will thrive and bloom their heads off if given the chance. I left full of ideas and also a new sense of freedom to sometimes let nature run its course, while I watch and observe.

Probably the most heartwarming characteristic of English gardening is the simplest: People in the British Isles love to garden. In the United States, many people think of gardening as a chore or at least a labor they don't have time for. When we show people around our very much in-progress garden at the Cape and describe what we have planned for the future, the reaction is usually, "What a lot of work." They're not wrong. The work is the point of it. The very act of gardening is beloved in the UK. It is their national pastime.

The English fixation on gardening allows garden magazines there to continue to publish, where so many have shuttered here. One of my favorite stress-relieving television shows, *Gardeners' World,* has been on the air since 1968. The program features gardeners from all walks of life in all kinds of settings: chic city gardens, country showplaces, community gardens, historic estates, and ordinary backyards, which are often self-filmed by their owners on their phones. My favorite guests on the show are the holders of the National Plant Collections. These are officially designated people or organizations whose goal is to collect and nurture as many hybrids and species of a specific group of plants as humanly possible. As you might imagine, the collection holders tend to be charmingly hyper-focused on their plant groups in an eccentrically British way. There are around seven hundred collections, many of which are open to the public, ranging from the abutilon (flowering maple) collection in Herefordshire to the zingiber (ornamental ginger) collection in Edinburgh. The goal is to preserve as many plant varieties as possible for posterity.

Unlike gardeners in the British Isles, our country is vast with widely disparate climates and horticultural zones. What works in Vermont doesn't usually work in Southern California. In the UK, the Gulf Stream keeps the weather milder and more temperate, though their climate is changing rapidly and unexpectedly too: more heat and drought in midsummer, more cold and wet in the winter.

When I was a kid on those trips to the UK, I walked around as if I were in horticultural heaven. I didn't think about being a gardener at the time, though I enjoyed doing it at home with my parents. The beauty of the plants and flowers captivated me. For months afterward, I drew scenes from the trip with colored pencils, like the giant historic rhododendrons we saw in the walled garden at Warwick Castle. I also sketched out imaginary historic houses and grounds and drew mazes like the one we got lost in at Hampton Court.

Seeing London's gated squares and parks dense with shrubberies and tangled vines reminded me of the eerie feeling of mystery and discovery I'd found in children's books set in the UK, such as Francis Hodgson Burnett's *The Secret Garden,* C. S. Lewis's *The Chronicles of Narnia,* and Joan Aiken's *The Wolves of Willoughby Chase.* As an adult, I recognize the nostalgia and propagandization of what "being British" might mean, and how it's been used strategically over the course of the British Empire period and beyond. But I notice something when watching contemporary programs, such as *The Great British Bake Off,* that reflect the diverse Britain of today. Everybody, no matter their national origin, seems to enjoy the ritual of a cuppa and a sticky toffee pudding or Victoria sponge. The garden equivalent might be a cottage garden with a hollyhock-flanked gate. Or a giant herbaceous flower border. The common thread of all these examples of the English garden is imagination, centuries of it, and a love of horticulture. Both of which can inspire just as much creativity on our side of the Atlantic. But since we're not an island nation, there will be some bigger adjustments for the hard freezes, heat, and drought that our continental weather gives us.

OVERLEAF, LEFT (*clockwise from top left*): A quiet corner at Charleston Farmhouse. The new walled garden at Knepp Castle. A long vista at Sissinghurst. A row of irises at Charleston Farmhouse.

OVERLEAF, RIGHT: Sissinghurst's distinctive garden rooms viewed from the tower.

THROUGH A GARDEN LENS

I photograph my garden almost every day during the growing season. I try to walk through each morning, looking closely at what might make a good image. What plants are blooming, or budding up, or fading gorgeously. Sometimes I use my serious camera, a Canon EOS R6, and sometimes I just grab shots on the fly with my phone because a bird just alighted on a trellis or a bee is tussling with a lavender spike. Taking photos has become my visual journal. If I need to check when the anemones bloomed last spring or I want to see what bloomed three years ago in a border, all I have to do is go check the date in my phone's photo library. Capturing moments from your garden is pure creativity, and at the same time, a document for you as the gardenmaker. During my magazine years, I learned from many talented individuals the best ways to photograph gardens, and as you'd imagine, it's all about the light, especially at the beginning or end of the day.

I've watched dawn arrive in gardens around the world. As garden editor at *House & Garden, Domino,* and *Martha Stewart Living,* my job was to travel with photographers to document all types of gardens, from intimate backyards to grand estates. It was thrilling to arrive at a house before dawn, stealthily letting ourselves into the garden to avoid waking up the homeowner. And then, if it was a clear sky, to get the rush of watching the sun illuminate the plants and design of the spaces. Because the best garden photography almost always occurs

Backlit alliums, culver's root, sanguisorba, and hollyhocks.

in the first and last hours of the day, the photography crew had to get up very early. In some parts of the world, it could mean awakening before four a.m. I know that's not hard for some; for me, it was a disaster. But it was worth the effort as I got to see some of the most beautiful gardens in the world as they woke up.

My job was not to take the photographs. It was to help the photographer tell the story visually. The process was as delicate and collaborative as a dance. I worked with many of the great editorial photographers of the latter part of the twentieth century and first part of the twenty-first. They would follow the light, which is the key to creating a good garden or landscape photograph. The light will point you to the shot, but it's more about where you stand in reference to the sun that makes all the difference.

I learned from the French photographer Alexandre Bailhache how to photograph *contre-jour* ("against the day"), which is the poetically French word for "backlit" or, technically, "against the light." In this method, the sun is behind the subject of the image, whether it's a flower head or a flower bed, and the photographer aims toward the light source. Shooting this way gives a sense of shape and a painterly sense of depth. Conversely, photographing with frontal light can often flatten a subject. Alex also had a technique where he would crouch very low so that the camera lens peered through flowers into another space: alliums in the foreground of a kitchen garden, for instance. If you want to show the romance of your garden, use the low blocking technique to add a little mystery. I call this shot the "forgiving oblique" because it hides a multitude of sins. If you want to document the design, then get up on a ladder or higher spot to show how the various spaces interconnect.

At Great Dixter, Christopher Lloyd and Fergus Garrett's garden masterpiece in England, Alex and I arrived in a deluge. Alex was undeterred, and I held the umbrella over him while we photographed through the large drops. He knew that the rain, which in this case was backed by a fairly light-filled sky rather than a dark gloomy one, would add something so wonderful that it would be well worth how wet we would get by the end. Those special weather moments—fog, mist, dew, hoarfrost, snow, the soft pink light of dawn, the flaming light of a sunset—are all conditions that make an arresting image.

One of my most memorable garden shoots was photographing two large estate gardens designed by Fernando Caruncho along Spain's Costa Brava. At the time, New York–based photographer Dana Gallagher worked with a large format wooden field camera. It produced film that was 4 by 5 inches (most of these photo shoots I'm mentioning were pre-digital). The camera was a bulky object to maneuver and travel with despite being pretty light. One had to know which images they were seeking because the film and processing were expensive. It was imperative to look and make firm decisions to get it right the first time.

I stood with Dana at sunset in an expanse of lavender about half the size of a football field at a private estate in Spain. The sunlight was long, low, and soft—ideal for a photo shoot. We stood among the honeybees, who seemed almost as intoxicated as we were by the scent of the thousands of lavender blossoms that surrounded us. I photographed many gardens with Dana and her "magic camera" as I called it. She taught me about f-stops and depth of field, when to make a sharp image and when to let some of the photograph be soft and out-of-focus to add a little mystery.

Back in the States, I often worked with Marion Brenner at a number of California gardens. I remember how much I enjoyed my first annual spring trips there in early March when it was cold and dreary back east but well into spring on the West Coast. As I headed to Napa or Sonoma, the scents of eucalyptus trees along the road wafted in through the open car windows, just as the dawn notes of jasmine, lavender, and society garlic would drift through the gardens we photographed. As a longtime Berkeley resident, Marion is an expert on local flora, especially the varieties that only grow in California, which were new to me.

Marion also taught me about angles, both high and low. One aspect of my job was to suggest possible shots to the photographer, most importantly when the light was moving quickly at sunrise and sunset. While she was shooting in one area, I would dart around as the light moved somewhere else, or I'd go look for where other beautiful shots might be occurring, some lasting only a few minutes. The first and last parts of a shoot day, then, were intense and fun as we tried to be everywhere at once. She and I are about a foot apart in height, so occasionally when I would point out a potential shot, she'd reply, "I don't see it." But she did when I grabbed her step stool. While at other times, she'd see a shot I didn't see—that is, until I bent down a bit. It was good for a laugh and as a reminder that we all see things from our particular perspectives. Sometimes the best angle is not at eye level. You have to get up, or go down, to find it.

The best photographs capture how it feels to be in a garden—the mood, the atmosphere, the energy that exists only in that place. Ngoc Minh Ngo, another photographer I love to work with, infuses her photographs with such a high level of that ineffable quality that to look at her work is to be transported to the space—so much so you practically feel the moisture coming off the plants as the summer air cools and the evening's scents start to unspool. After working with her on several shoots, I came to believe it's her patience and ability to wait for just the right moment, that combination of light and atmosphere that makes a photograph memorable.

One of the biggest cultural changes that's occurred between my days working with these photographers and today is that smartphones allow everyone to create relatively decent images. The capability has created an uncountable number of images swirling around the internet and social media. Though we sometimes cluster annoyingly around a gorgeous sunset, or a world-famous work of art, aren't we all developing the same skills, seeing what images will flatten into a good composition or what angles or light will give the best result? I hear folks criticize our modern cameras-out culture as creating a sense that people are no longer really seeing what's around them but, instead, looking distractedly through their phones. But I would counter that argument by saying that photography creates a formalized way to focus our gaze and see aspects of our gardens that would otherwise be easy to overlook. I view the photographic practice I have not only as a tool for both the design of my garden, but also as a valuable creative outlet—and we all need a few more of those.

LESSON

HOW TO PHOTOGRAPH YOUR GARDEN

Digital and smartphone cameras become more sophisticated each year. Here are some tips that I've discovered over the years that give me the best results.

- Photograph during the lower light levels of dawn or sunset rather than in the middle of day. Midday sun flattens shapes, especially when directly overhead.
- Experiment with photographing with backlighting to reveal the shapes of the plants. If soft light is hitting the edges of flowers or leaves, the backlit effect will add that touch of magic.
- The photographic technique known as "flare" is related to backlighting but allows the low sun at sunset or sunrise to actually shine into the lens so that a soft halo of sun is visible. Experiment with the technique by blocking a bit of the light hitting the edge of your lens with your free hand.
- The warmish-pink light at either end of the day adds a romantic feeling to a photograph. Mist or morning ground fog creates magical photos, even if they seem a bit overcast. If you have ground fog that becomes illuminated by the sun, then you've really hit the jackpot.
- To capture a flower close-up, put your phone near the object but zoom in even more tightly, using a pinching motion on the phone screen. This will create falloff in the depth of field so that your object is in focus while the background is blurrier, an effect called "bokeh." If you're using a professional camera, there are more precise ways to obtain this.

A busy tangle of larkspurs and poppies benefits from a shallower depth of field.

THE SUBTLE ART OF SHADE

Over the years, I've come to appreciate the more subdued charms of a shade garden. The woodland-loving plants that thrive with little sun may seem modest and even a bit shy. But as I've matured as a gardener, I've discovered that a well-chosen shade planting can contain more visual detail and interest than a sunny herbaceous flower bed. Such grand sun-loving statements are meant to be viewed from afar with blocks of color arranged in drifts. Shade gardens ask to be looked at close-up. Their complex leaf patterns and variegation open the eyes in a different way.

My conversion was partly due to necessity. The tree canopy in two of our former gardens made sun-loving plants an impossibility. The area around our upstate New York lake cabin was mossy and dense with shade from beeches and hemlocks. Though beautifully sylvan, it was not great for gardening. Not only because of the lack of sun, but also due to the heavy clay soil and army of deer that patrolled the neighborhood. I think my only shade garden successes on our half-acre were foxgloves (which are poisonous). Everything else was gobbled up.

Our next garden in an old neighborhood in Des Moines was better suited to grow a wider range of shade species. It was blessed with several towering ash trees, so to plant under them, I had to adjust my vision and come up with new concepts that didn't include as many

In my previous garden in Des Moines, Iowa, I created a shade bed of leaf patterns and subtle colors.

sun-loving flowers. I learned to pay more attention to leaf color, pattern, and the finely wrought intricacies of tiny, graceful flowers. Shade gardening is for connoisseurs of subtlety, and there is a real artistry in leaning into that.

The previous homeowners had tried to solve the problem of what would grow in the roots underneath the tall ashes by going plantless. They covered the area with vivid colors of crushed stone, but I knew I wanted to do something less harsh-looking, something softer and greener. It was a garden, not a shopping center parking lot, after all. Removing the stone and torn landscape fabric underneath was a dusty job. When I finally cleared the area, I was disappointed to find exactly what I had expected—hardpan soil and a thick web of tree roots.

Over the following weeks, I carefully dug around the tree's massive roots and loosened up the earth wherever I could successfully wedge in a trowel, while adding compost and soil conditioners to support the new plantings. My research focused on identifying species beyond pachysandra or ivy that could tolerate the dry shade conditions under the tree. There were already a few existing hostas (the basic green ones) but nothing else of interest. I had to let go of my fixation on flowers and explore foliage textures and patterns—all the possible options for streaks, lines, veins, spots, and striations. I scoured the local nurseries and landed on a mix of low-growing perennials I hoped might brighten up the front walk. It turned out to be one of my most rewarding gardening successes and I discovered a whole new palette of plants in the process, some of which do have exceptional blooms as well as decorative leaves.

I rarely tell casual acquaintances about my obsession with lungworts, unless of course they ask for advice on shade gardening. These perennials are most known for their handsome leaves, which are spotted and lung-shaped; hence their genus name *Pulmonaria.* They are a standout choice for most any shade garden. I knew about the leaves before growing them but had no idea of the magnificence of their flowers, which start off in a range of pinks or reds and then, over a few days, turn bluish-purple. The process is a pollinator-attraction strategy that occurs as the pH levels shift blossom by blossom, causing a dynamic visual effect as they change. The color range is thought to direct pollinators toward newer, more nectar-rich reddish-pink flowers and away from older blue flowers. Other members of the borage (Boraginaceae) family, including borage itself, forget-me-nots, viper's bugloss, and Virginia bluebells, show this variability in color between pink and blue, and they have distinctively curving flower heads referred to as scorpioid cymes. Noticing the shifts between the fluid purple shades is one of those understated charms that can turn any gardener into a shadenista. The leaf colors are there for the rest of the growing season after the spring flowers depart. I'm partial to the silver, almost white-leaved lungworts, like 'Moonshine', 'Diana Clare', or 'Opal', that brighten the shade and glow at dusk.

Along with the lungworts, I planted lamium or dead nettles, a plant group that could use some name rebranding. There is wide variation in their bicolor white/silver and green patterned foliage, ranging from stripes to brushy strokes, the most common of which is 'White Nancy'. The crinkled leaf texture and square stems identify these plants as belonging to the vast mint family. And, like mint, they can spread easily but aren't as aggressive. Under a tree, they performed as I wanted them to—filling the space with their graphic leaves and pink, white, or purple flowers. Another lamium species, yellow archangel (*L. galeobdolon*), has similar leaves but bears yellow flowers.

Continuing the silver and green leaf theme, I grew several hybrids of Siberian bugloss (*Brunnera macrophylla*), which have large white or silver-tinged leaves and sky-blue flowers that resemble clouds of forget-me-nots. I kept going with the Midwestern native American alumroot (*Heuchera americana*). Its jade- and white-marbled foliage that sometimes has a hint of eggplant purple blended in well with the other leaf and flower colors. These plants perform in dry shade (always a tricky spot), as do the whorled leaves of sweet woodruff (*Galium odoratum*). The latter's fragrant star-shaped flowers are traditionally dried to flavor May wine. Whenever I could find them at nurseries, I added wild gingers, both the Chinese type (*Asarum splendens*) that are patterned with symmetrical silver on their dark green leaves that remind me of inkblot tests and the emerald-leaved North American species (*A. canadense*).

I couldn't resist including delicate white flowers like bleeding hearts, star-of-Bethlehem, and spring Grecian windflowers that bloom early but disappear by June. I needed something easy and inexpensive to fill the gaps the spring ephemerals left behind, so I reached back into my childhood and reconsidered caladiums. I hadn't thought much about them since I was a kid, when my dad and I planted them along a side yard. They grew robustly, loving the heat and humidity of the central Iowa summers and putting on a big street-facing show for the neighbors. I probably ordered too many, tempted by the wide range of graphic leaf patterns I found at several specialty online nurseries. However, I did show some discipline by avoiding any pink tones and sticking to my silver, green, and white color scheme, leaning into the almost solid white varieties, such as 'Moonlight', 'Candidum Sr.', and 'White Marble'.

Much of my planting ideas came from public or private gardens I photographed over the years, but I was also inspired by the shade garden of my former boss Martha Stewart at her Bedford, New York, home. She created a jewel box of a garden underneath a stand of tall trees behind one of her houses. Each plant bears close inspection, but she masterfully put them in large groups, so the effect was lush and cohesive. Some of the unusual varieties I remember are the tropical-looking shredded umbrella plant (*Syneilesis aconitifolia*) and the native may-apple (*Podophyllum peltatum*) with its white flowers that nod demurely under the palmate leaves. A big patch of large-flowered bellwort (*Uvularia grandiflora*) bobbed in the breeze with yellow bell-shaped flowers next to trout lilies and various ferns. Solomon's seal (*Polygonatum odoratum*) that, like the may-apple and bellwort, had hidden or drooping flowers that drew pollinators from below while protecting themselves from nibbling herbivores above.

We have recently taken some of these lessons to the Cape, where our property is primarily sunny. Last year, Chad cleared a wooded area alongside the driveway that was previously choked by black cherry saplings and invasive bush honeysuckle. There, under a canopy of black locusts and oaks, we put in spring bulbs, hellebores, ferns, and foxgloves the first year. This year, our goal has been to focus more on native shade species, many of which we've found at very reasonable bare-root prices online. I'm particularly pleased with the native cranesbill (*Geranium maculatum*) with its pale lilac flowers, which arrive in waves over several weeks in the early summer. Hardy geraniums of all sorts, which are not the tender geraniums (more properly *Pelargoniums*) that you see as summer bedding plants, are essential in a part-shade garden for their long flowering period. We also included amsonia, bowman's root (*Gillenia trifoliata*), wild sweet William (*Phlox maculata*), and a range of trilliums and wood anemones that will keep the beds interesting from spring till frost. We also added several witch hazel trees for winter and early spring interest, as well as understory shrubs like my favorite sweetfern (*Comptonia peregrina*) that grows wild in our local woods. It is neither sweet nor a fern, but instead a short woody bush with fern-like leaves that smell woodsy and spicy enough that I'm surprised no one has ever captured its scent to perfume soap or fragrance.

As I continue to experiment with new plants and take note of ones that work and why, my connection to shade gardening grows. It's true, abundant sun opens up a wider range of plant options, but once you dip into the enigmatic world of shade you might never want to come back into the light.

OVERLEAF, LEFT (*clockwise from top left*): Star-of-Bethlehem; Lunaria 'Corfu Blue'; Lungwort; Hellebore.

OVERLEAF, RIGHT: Frosty blue Siberian bugloss (Brunnera macrophylla) and 'Silver Bay' hosta.

THE RESILIENCE OF PANSIES

I never used to pay much attention to pansies. On our New York City rooftop, I planted only the small-flowered purple and yellow variety called johnny-jump-up or heartsease. Plant snobs considered them somehow more tasteful than the flouncy big-faced pansies at the garden center and, full confession, I felt the same. But since I started gardening on the Cape a couple of years ago, I find myself falling hard for pansies—the flouncier, the louder, the better.

Life can be difficult for plants in my sandy Cape Cod garden. We are well into our second year of springtime drought. Bracing north winds sweep over from the ocean-facing Back Shore with great regularity. The only gardeners are my husband and me. All these factors demand species that are tough and independent. Little did I know that one of my most stalwart successes would be the diminutive members of the viola clan. After my first season of planting six-packs from the garden center, pansies now self-seed everywhere: between paving stones, underneath hoses, in the lawn, smack in the middle of the gravel. Some even make it through our milder winters in sheltered spots, nodding off after the first frost and waking up as temperatures climb.

Along with scented violets, pansies are in the genus *Viola,* a large group of plants with deep historical associations. In the language of flowers, heartsease or wild pansies (*Viola tricolor*) say "think of me." During the Tudor period, they were used in love potions and associated with the idea of missing, or longing for, a beloved. An eleven-year-old Elizabeth I embroidered a book with heartsease for her beloved stepmother Katherine Parr, the only wife to survive Henry VIII. Later, as queen, Elizabeth was often painted in several of her official portraits with embroidered pansies on her garments.

Why have violas, especially pansies, been linked with the idea of thought for so many years? The name pansy comes from the French word for thinking, "penser." A commonly reported etymological theory is that most pansies sport faces that look like they are scrunched up in deep thought—the kind of face you make when you are really trying to remember something. The large-flowered hybrids don't exist in nature; they are the outcome of intense plant breeding by competing aristocrats in nineteenth-century England, reaching their height of popularity later in the century. Though Victorians have a reputation for social conservatism, they liked their pansies big, bright, and blowsy with as many blotches, cross-hatching, ruffles, picotees, and color combos as possible.

Could this quality of defiant flamboyance have contributed to the usage of "pansy" as an anti-gay slur? In the early- to mid-twentieth century, several flower names were used as insults for gay or gender nonconforming men, including buttercups (which had a resurgence recently as "suck it up, buttercup"), daffodils, and lilies (as in the related term "lily-livered"). Pansy is, after all, not one of the worst epithets, and any member of the LGBTQ community, me included, can likely tell you exactly when and where they were when they've had such insults lobbed at us over the years.

I like pansies for their patterning and nearly full-spectrum color range. And growing them over the past several years has given me a new appreciation for how unstoppable they are when they find a place they like. They are weeds you want, and I give them full rein. Under all the flounces and stylish colors (this year I'm really into the pinky-mauvy-browns and the ruffles of the 'Frizzle Sizzle' or 'Rococo' series), I admire their innate fierceness and resolute but cheerful will to survive. Anybody who chooses to live on this windy, sandy, stormy spit of land jutting out in the Atlantic can probably identify. Let's just say, never underestimate the toughness of a pansy.

In the long border, fall arrives on the Cape with cooler air and an explosion of hardy 'Sheffield' chrysanthemums.

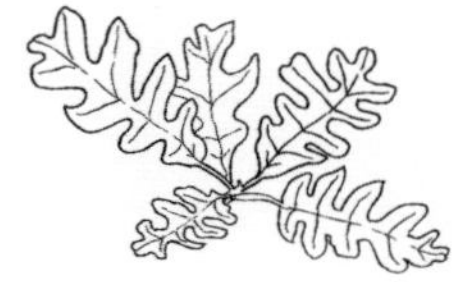

A CERTAIN SLANT OF LIGHT

In much of the country, spring and fall are the most fleeting seasons and, for me, the most precious. I love spring because each day the sun sets later, and the garden becomes more floriferous as we gather momentum daily on the way to high summer. In autumn, I ration the clear, warmish days and cool nights at the end of the growing season the way I savor the final bites of a dish I'm particularly enjoying. To prolong the feeling, I try to use all my senses to capture what's subtly morphing around me.

Sometime in the afternoon on late August days, I'll notice a slight shift in the angle of the sunlight and realize fall is returning—almost as if I had forgotten it would come. The moment makes me stop whatever I'm doing and pay attention. The atmosphere surrounding the clouds is a little clearer and bluer instead of humid and golden. As the leaves brown, I notice the sweet scent of their sugars and organic compounds as they decompose. It's a fragrance we get only for a few weeks in October. The marigolds and hardy chrysanthemums I've fallen in love with over the past few years float a spicy, honeyed, bittersweet fragrance over the garden. The first waft of woodsmoke from a neighbor's fireplace makes me feel both cozy and excited, but it also gives me a little tug of dread about the upcoming plant-less winter. As Emily Dickinson wrote in her lyric poem "There's a certain Slant of light" about the visible shift of the seasons: "When it comes, the Landscape listens—Shadows—hold their breath."

Dickinson was writing about winter, but the title runs through my head as I notice the first signs that early autumn is announcing the inevitable arrival of colder temperatures. The sounds of nature quicken in the chill after the cicadas' languid drone dies down. There's an urgent whisper coming from the tree branches as the leaves become papery, while the pollinators rush from flower to flower before packing it up for the year. In the woods behind our house, I hear the eerie late-night whinnies and trills of the eastern screech owls, unseen but watching everything as they call to one another. In the distance, coyotes trade banshee wails among packs. The sound of the waves gains strength as more frequent storms erode the high Atlantic dunes. It's still warm enough for me to swim in the freshwater kettle ponds back in the woods in the morning and in the bay at Herring Cove when there's an afternoon high tide. Still, the flora and fauna around us sound like they're preparing for something big and urgent after a summer respite. Speaking for myself, however, by the time autumn rolls around I am ready to stop the ceaseless mowing, planting, trimming, and weeding. Granted, there are still end-of-season tasks to do, but the obsessive pull of the garden seems to wane after Labor Day. As the nights cool and lengthen and the sun weakens, the plants decline and start to look a bit tired. But even surrounded by all this decline, I prefer to go out with a big autumnal bang.

Ever since I was a beginner gardener, I've planted for a dramatic finish. On my Chelsea rooftop, I didn't want to waste even one week of the growing season. I began adding such late-season stars as Japanese anemones, asters, ornamental grasses, and Montauk daisies to my containers. One of my major influences at the time was the 1990 book *The Garden in Autumn* by Allen Lacy. Previously I had thought of fall as a grand horticultural exhale ending in a collapse on the couch (though I might have been projecting). I found, however, that with thoughtful planting, the opposite is true and you can steer your garden into early winter on a crescendo.

By August in my Cape Cod garden, I can see the tiny silver buds on the small shrubby bluebeard (*Caryopteris*) that will become electric blue flowers in late September. The Japanese anemones are starting to open their velvet knob-like buds. The low-growing stems of leadwort (*Ceratostigma plumbaginoides*) are covered with flowers the color of a

French blue button-down shirt. I wait till the last minute to gather my herbs, aiming to let them grow as large as possible. Fall's signature herbs are the woody varieties: rosemary, sage, thyme, and winter savory, but I make sure to gather every bit of my tender anise hyssop, lavender, lemon verbena, marjoram, and mint to dry before they're cut down by frost. Near the front driveway and in the long border, the hardy chrysanthemums I planted in the spring (focusing on the Korean and Rubellum varieties for their loose, graceful growing habits and soft colors) burst into flower. The lavenders, trailing petunias, and overgrown alyssum that I cut back in midsummer reward me with a fall repeat bloom. And, of course, there are all the shrubs and trees, such as oaks and serviceberries, which exhibit dynamic leaf color as they head into winter.

Spring has always been the harbinger of new life, new year, new growth. I feel something similar when I plant a late-blooming variety early in the season. I know it will step forward with a jolt of color just as other characters in my little garden play are bowing out. As someone who doesn't much like the quiescence of winter (I enjoy growing plants too much), that one last burst gives me something to look forward to. I make a point to visit the nurseries weekly in autumn to take advantage of end-of-season sales and to check out what is blooming from September through November. These are the plants that will carry me to the brink of winter. I also keep an eye out for colorful native plants on view in our local woods or neighborhoods.

As Maya Angelou once explained in a television interview, "Once I really admitted that I would die. That is the one promise I can be sure will not be reneged upon. Once I understood that, then I could be present. And I'm totally present all the time." Brief as it is, autumn is about big themes: change, transformation, decline, hibernation, death, the promise of rebirth in spring—all wrapped up in a climax of some of the most vivid colors, scents, and flavors of the calendar. This fall, let's plan to celebrate this fleeting season before the cold and snow arrives, if you still get any. I think we all benefit from not letting its charms, both modest and exuberant, pass by unnoticed.

The view over the little bluestem in the front yard, a rare remnant of Cape Cod's sandplain meadows.

Bees pay many visits to aster 'Purple Dome'.

OPPOSITE: Dahlias, rangy so late in the season, look out over a foggy meadow.

SALAD BOXES

When we first moved into our Cape house in early March, the landscape was bare and monotonous except for shades of browns, grays, and a deep evergreen. In retrospect, it was the perfect time to see a new house and garden, stripped down to its winter studs. I could see the structure of the trees and hedges, both evergreen and bare, and not be distracted by the garden in full leaf and flower. I wandered the property in those early days feeling very excited but a little overwhelmed, wondering what plants were sleeping out there and what we might successfully add in the future. With spring just around the corner, I wanted to begin as soon as possible.

I looked back to memories of my previous gardens and my "salad boxes" came to mind. When I lived in Des Moines, I had an elevated back deck outside the kitchen door where I wanted to put an edible garden. I bought three large wooden planters that were about six-by-three-by-three feet and filled them with potting soil and compost. Then, in the still wintry April of Zone 5 Iowa, I direct-seeded hardier greens: Asian mustards, spinach, and lettuce, especially the winter cultivars that are selected to be cold hardy. Over the next months, I harvested wave after wave of salad greens, herbs, and edible flowers. It is one of life's greatest pleasures to walk outside with a wooden salad bowl and come back in the kitchen a few minutes later with twenty or more types of edible plant leaves and flowers. Not only

Summer months are filled with homegrown salads.

is it more beautiful to look at than a plate of green leaves, but the variation in nutrition from the different plants with their leaf colors is better than a fistful of vitamin pills. The back terrace in Iowa was fairly high so the rampant deer population and any random rabbits were kept at bay. Chipmunks and ground squirrels (in Des Moines they are nicknamed squinnies), acrobatic enough to climb into the boxes, didn't cause much real damage.

Though I had never gardened in Cape Cod, I realized my salad boxes might well work as raised beds instead of planters. There was a large rectangular space outlined by privet hedges right outside the back door of the screen porch, which would be perfect for a kitchen garden except that a giant silver maple tree cast shade over that area. But directly next to this shady space was the sun-filled former dog run with its mixture of gravel and rough grass. This worked as a space for the raised beds because I didn't yet know we would transform that space into a gravel garden. Not knowing what the ultimate layout of our property would be, I decided raised beds would work well as a temporary solution where I could grow vegetables without committing to something permanent. So I devised something solid—effective in its purpose but easy to dismantle when we decided to move them where they would ultimately go.

The four raised beds were supported by metal corners from a mail-order source in heights ranging from six to twelve inches into which I hammered two-inch boards with a rubber mallet. The boards can be as long as you need to create a rectangle that you fill with soil. The beauty of these open frames is that two people can easily lift and move them if needed. For that first spring, I knew I wanted to grow vegetables and herbs so I began with hardy salad greens in those first chilly spring weeks, just as I had in Iowa. By summer's end, everything was going well until the eventful fall day when the maple fell during a Halloween nor'easter. After clearing up the remains of the limbs, we relocated the beds to their proper home, the place we had originally wanted them outside the back door. Chad and I carried them over to their new spot and filled them up with new soil and started again the following spring, minus a grand tree but with plenty of available sun.

Over the past three years, I've experimented with dozens of edible greens. I've found that these varieties perform well in my Zone 7B location where the springs are cool until June, and the summers can be dry and hot into mid-August. Many of these also did well in Des Moines, with very cold winters and hot, humid summers. Most greens are very adaptable but prefer cooler weather over blistering heat, so pick your planting window accordingly. Warmer climate gardeners in the South or Southern California grow them in fall, winter, or spring, while northerners get best results in spring and early summer through fall, with a break during the hot temperatures of late July.

One of my staple greens is spicy arugula (*Eruca vesicaria*), which, now commonplace, has many names and variations. Long popular in Europe, it's called rocket in England, rucola or ruchetta in Italy, and roquette in France. Craig Claiborne is credited with introducing arugula in a *New York Times* article dated May 24, 1960, under the lead "Pungent Ingredient Is Cause of Confusion for City Shopper." He mentions several familiar aspects of the plant: its sharp flavor, its sandiness, and its value as a "secret ingredient" in restaurant salads of the period. He also gives a recipe for Rocket Canapes I'm going to try: finely chopped arugula mixed with garlic or a scallion, Tabasco, lemon juice, and a little mayonnaise served on bread rounds. There are many hybrids to choose from. All are easy to grow by direct-sowing them on top of the soil. The names of the various types and leaf shapes seem to be kind of mixed up in the trade. The emerald green, softer-leaved hybrids like 'Astro' are the most classic. The darker, more deeply lobed "wild" types, such as 'Sylvetta', sometimes known as 'Selvatica Rucola', tend to be spicier. The hybrid called 'Wasabi' tends to be the hottest of them all, just stopping short of rushing a blast up your nose like its namesake.

There's another type of arugula on the Outer Cape, or maybe it's the same as the wild types listed above, though it seems even more narrow-leaved with wirier stems and profuse yellow flowers that self-seed everywhere. *Diplotaxis tenuifolia* is sometimes referred to as wild rocket or perennial wallrocket, but around here some people refer to it as rustica. It is perennial, though it's difficult to differentiate between the plants that live more than a season and those that self-seed. I never planted rustica, but I have it as a welcome guest in my raised beds. It might have come in with a soil delivery. It's delicious when picked young, but the ruffled leaves become spicier and even bitter if left on the plant too long over the season. It's so tenacious that I see it growing out of the sidewalk cracks along the main street in nearby Provincetown.

Asian greens and mustards are, along with arugula, one of the earliest plants I direct-sow, starting in late March to mid-April. They can handle the cold as tiny seedlings and, once in full leaf, survive temperatures into the twenties or lower, in my well-draining soil. As with many plants, winter drainage is as important as temperatures for their survival. I first tasted their spicy leaves in mesclun, the leafy mix that became popular in the 1980s and is now in every produce aisle. What you buy in a plastic clamshell is a pale imitation of the vibrancy that will come from your garden. I always get a few mesclun or mustard seed mixes to grow in addition to individual varieties like 'Ruby Streaks' and 'Golden Frills'. Both are aptly named and add bold color and texture to salads. Frilly green mizuna has a milder, almost perfumy, flavor. Larger mustards like 'Vibrant Ultraviolet', 'Dragon Tongue' (also known as 'Ho Mi Z'), and 'Red Giant' are vibrant salad additions when young but better sautéed as the large leaves age. The latter is such a striking dark red and so long-lasting in leaf that I've grown it in the flower border as an ornamental that happens to be edible.

Lettuce, when homegrown, may look as delicate as tissue paper but it's surprisingly tough and cold hardy, even to the point of lightly freezing before bouncing back to life after a thaw. Heirloom varieties have very little resemblance to the red or green leaf lettuces, 'Romaine' or 'Iceberg', that populate most supermarket shelves. Those sturdy lettuces are built to withstand the long journey from California's Central Valley to faraway places like the outer tip of Cape Cod. The closest supermarket variety to what I like to grow at home is 'Butter' or 'Boston' lettuce that has to be protected in a polyethylene dome. I felt guilty for buying the single-use plastic, but now I am using the containers as mini seed-starting greenhouses. I look for the most delicate lettuces, oak-leaved hybrids like 'Flashy Lightning' or tall-leaved cob lettuces like 'Forellenschluss' (a.k.a. 'Speckled Trout'). It helps that many have interesting visual features, such as spots, streaks, or gradations of maroon, yellows, and greens. I'm a sucker for the names: 'Merveille de Quatre Saisons' (a French Bibb lettuce), 'Mayan Jaguar', 'Maule's Philadelphia Butter', or 'Les Oreilles du Diable' ('Devil's Ear'). If you really want to push the season either in the spring or fall, look for hybrids whose names indicate they are unusually cold hardy, such as 'Landis Winter', 'Reine des Glaces' ('Ice Queen'), or the Amish variety 'Eva Snader's Brown Winter Lettuce'. Growing a wide variety of lettuces is a gardening essential for me. Any salad I make during the growing season starts with their beautifully textured and colored leaves as a base for more assertive flavors.

Other greens that too easily catch my eye in the catalogs include a very soft early broccoli raab called 'Spring Raab', so sweet and delicate you can eat it raw. It's not comparable to the often tough raab (rapini) found in the grocery store. As a vegetable, raab is more closely related to turnips and bok choy than it is to broccoli. The name derives from its broccoli-like florets. I once planted mâche (corn salad or lamb's lettuce) and now have it forevermore; it self-seeds that readily. The small rosettes of leaves are delicately flavored. French sorrel, a hardy perennial, is not delicately flavored at all with its biting, mouth-puckering tang of lemon and should be used sparingly in salads. It is very nice raw in a cold soup with yogurt or in a *potage Germiny*, a classic hot French soup with broth and cream. Upland cress, with a flavor reminiscent of watercress, is another low-growing salad green that can be weedy, but still nutty and delicious.

Classic spinach is, once again, a plant I can't grow enough of. As any cook knows, a giant pile of spinach sautés down to almost nothing. I'm not sure I've ever heard someone say, "Oops, I cooked too much spinach." Look for varieties like 'Bloomsdale Long Standing' or 'Steadfast Hardy' that you can plant as early as possible in later winter (or very early spring) so that you have weeks of harvest before the summer heat causes the cool-loving plants to bolt (or go to seed).

Salad herbs add that little grace note of flavor. Used with a light touch, a little tarragon, dill, lemon thyme, or mint (though never peppermint, which adds an unfortunate toothpaste taste) gives something almost imperceptible to the mix. Similar to a pleasant association that lives in your subconscious. I enjoy chervil for the same reason. It goes in almost all my salads with its fine, faint anise flavor. Flat-leaved, mineral-green Italian parsley sneaks in another undercurrent of flavor, but in this case it is sharper. Last, a few chopped chives, which I consider to be the subtlest of the onion clan, give a salad a grounding of allium flavor that is especially appetizing.

Plant in succession every couple of weeks in the spring so that you'll have a longer period to pick leaves. By mid-May, the baby seedlings will need to be thinned on a regular, if not daily, basis so that the plants can have space to grow larger. But don't think of it as a chore. You'll be eating your microgreens; some of them probably won't even make it into the salad before being nibbled straight from your hand. Grow lettuces either like mesclun, cutting off leaves as you need them, or let them form a head before cutting them off at the base to use as loose leaves or sliced in half and popped briefly on the grill. As the weather warms you may notice the lettuce starting to bolt by sending up a tall bloom spike. Harvest them before this happens; otherwise, the leaves will be irretrievably bitter—and I don't mean bitter like an endive. This bitterness will make you want to wash off your tongue with soap.

After all the spring greens have bolted or begun to wilt in the midsummer heat, I clear out the salad beds and put in vegetables that love the heat like tomatoes, eggplants, and peppers. I replace the spring pea vines on their twig support teepees with pole beans. Later, as the weather cools in late August, I sow another round for fall harvest. No space is wasted and, if all goes to plan, I have fresh produce to enjoy from late April to late December. The amount of work entailed is not enough to merit the title of homesteading, but I do feel proud and healthful every time I toss a salad that I grew myself.

Four raised beds provide produce from April to December in the Cape garden.

OPPOSITE (*clockwise from top left*): 'Sugar Magnolia' snap peas; 'French Breakfast' radishes; homegrown saffron; various salad greens.

Planter boxes and containers in Des Moines.

OWLS, RABBITS, COYOTES, AND TURKEYS

Most nights before going to bed, I make a point to head outside to look at the stars and stand still to listen for who I can hear in the woods. As I admire the constellations and wonder about the gaseous depths of the Milky Way I can see so clearly in the dark nights of the Outer Cape, I'm also listening. Several owls live in the woods around our house and, though I rarely see them, I treasure the times I can hear them. The low whinny of the screech owls most excites me. They have several sounds, but I usually hear what is called their "bounce song," a tremolo that goes something like *badabadabadabadabadabada.* Arcing up slightly before descending, the call allows mated pairs to keep track of one another in the forest. Their mysterious vocalizations evoke a slight shiver in me, though not from fear as these birds are only the size of a robin. When I hear them, I imagine what their lives are like. Ours are parallel. They, thinking about the things owls think about in their hollowed-out homes. And me, worrying about the things humans worry about. Both of us out under the gibbous moon.

When I catch sight of the moon, maybe while passing a window or when I go out in the backyard to look for it, I try to pause and make a wish. There's an old Billie Holiday song with lyrics by Dorothy

Bluebird boxes wait for this season's occupants in the meadow.

Parker that goes, "I wished on the moon for something I never knew. I wished on the moon for more than I ever knew. A sweeter rose, a softer sky. An April day that would not dance away." I make a game of it, never missing the opportunity to name a shortlist of things I hope will happen for me or people I care about. I am not usually superstitious, but I do believe in the grounding power of ritual. These little moonlit wishes, like all meditations, manifestations, mantras, and prayers, are exercises in intent.

I continue to hear and learn about other owls in the woods as well. I have never seen the tiniest one, the saw-whet owls, but I can hear them. I looked up online who could be making the quick *who-who-who-who* flute-like sound and was immediately charmed by their round cat-like faces and tiny bodies. I'll probably never see them in person, and I certainly don't want to disturb them. I enjoy knowing they are out there in the dark, keeping guard over the natural balance of rodents and rabbits.

The only owl I have seen on the property was truly a visitation. It felt like an apparition. One night I was in the kitchen and heard a loud call outside, the classic "*who*" an owl might make in a childhood cartoon—*hoo-h'HOO-hoo-hoo.* Chad and I opened the kitchen door and flicked on the porch light, expecting to see nothing. We found ourselves staring at a large great horned owl perched on a branch about ten feet from us. It was majestic, about two feet high. As we watched it, all three of us immobile, I heard a call from another owl farther back in the woods and the owl in my driveway turned its head around dramatically, stretched out giant wings that seemed to reach more than a yard wide, and flew off the branch, dipping down slightly with its full weight catching the air before gaining height as it flew up the driveway and off into the dark forest.

We do everything we can on our property to encourage and support wildlife. Our house sits in a little hollow that leads to a natural meadow of little bluestem grass in front of the house. I say we live in a bird bowl because of the number of species that frequent the trees and shrubs. We finally had a bluebird pair decide to make a home in the boxes Chad put up in the meadow specifically to entice them. The first year, we didn't see anything. The second year, a male selected a box but couldn't entice the female into a move-in, even after a lot of trying. The third season, he succeeded, and the pair hatched their nestlings. Hopefully they'll be back next year, even though the male was very territorial and repeatedly attacked our car. Thinking his reflection in our side window was a rival male, he showered the driver's window and mirror with poop in the most aggressive manner to defend his territory. Judging by all the mess, he seemed really upset.

Goldfinches visit the seed-bearing plants in the border and the meadow in posses. Woodpeckers carve out holes in the hard-as-concrete black locust trunks. Orioles swoop in to sip nectar from the apple blossoms in the spring, flashing cantaloupe orange as they dart among the shell-pink blossoms. A family of quail processes single file through our backyard like officials in a small parade. Rafters of turkeys, sometimes as many as a dozen, saunter through in the fall. The last native turkeys on the Cape were hunted to local extinction in the mid-nineteenth century, but in the 1990s they were reintroduced and made a big comeback. Some estimates put their population at 35,000. They don't do damage in my garden, but I have friends who dread the destruction they can wreak on a flower or vegetable bed as they scratch around looking for insects and worms.

Unlike our former homes in Iowa and upstate New York, we don't have many deer where we are. It might be the way the streets or highways bisect the forests of the Cape Cod National Seashore that surround us, or perhaps coyotes and coywolves are involved. According to a recent study, there are about eighty-one individuals just in our tiny Outer Cape. Before the last century they weren't here at all. I've only seen one deer in four years, but I've seen many coyotes and heard them even more often. Like the owls, their calls give me a chill, but in this case, there is the danger they pose to our pets and us. However, I respect them greatly. The way they sing their maniacal pack songs can sound as if they are agitated or upset, like they're having a fight, or copulating, or chasing something, or generally raising a fracas. Sometimes their barks more resemble those of dogs, like the coyote that once stood out in our yard and barked at the front door inexplicably for half an hour. I've seen them lope through our driveway, completely unconcerned with me. One moonless night, I heard their cacophony getting closer and closer until what sounded like a fairly large group of them stampeding right by the house as they chased prey, or one another, out into the dark.

Anything that keeps the hungry deer and rabbits at bay is fine by me, though I make sure to accompany our dog Pokey when he pops out for a quick pre-bedtime pee. The rabbits are my main problem when it comes to eating my plants. The first year, they didn't seem to know we were making a garden, but they have since found out and made up for their lapse over the subsequent growing seasons. Their main crime is eating my seed-sown annuals just as they become seedlings: cosmos, zinnias, maybe some poppies. The first year, I had an explosion of these plants, but last year, I barely saw one cosmos even though I scattered dozens of seed packets. This spring, I'm sowing my cosmos indoors and hoping the head start might help. I don't want to be forced to place chicken wire over my plants to allow them to grow past rabbit height, but I will do so if necessary.

Several red-tailed hawks often circle our property and are sometimes chased by a bullying murder of crows. I've seen a few dead bunny carcasses lying around, so I have my suspicions who the hunter is, but no proof. Recently, a large hawk chased a rabbit under our house near the front door and then hopped menacingly around the flower bed, waiting for it to come out. We waited too, looking from the window, but the rabbit didn't reappear and the hawk eventually lost interest. Hopefully these predators can help bring down the population a bit because my current practice of chasing rabbits around the yard and barking like a bloodhound doesn't seem to be doing the trick.

I cherish these wildlife interactions and the reminder they give to this place of its pre-human state. They were here before us, and even with our fences and chicken wire, we need to share. No matter how often I see a wild animal, be it a deer, a songbird, an owl, a coywolf, a quail, a fox—or, out on the water, a harbor seal, a mola mola, or a humpback whale—I am always a little surprised and constantly in awe. The only exceptions are rabbits—I see way too many of those.

LESSON

TIPS FOR SUPPORTING WILDLIFE

As natural areas become compromised by development and suburban encroachment, it's more important than ever for our properties to help close the gaps, even if it can seem like a drop in a big empty bucket. Mostly it's a mindset shift that's required. The following tips are a good place to begin.

- **Don't use rodenticide.** It's all too easy to reach for the mouse bait, but the household pests you're trying to rid yourself of end up going somewhere to die. Usually, out in the yard or garden where they can be eaten by predators like hawks and owls in the food chain, who then become poisoned and die too.
- **Dim or eliminate nighttime lighting.** Help nocturnal pollinators and birds hunt more effectively by allowing them the darkness that nature intended. If you are not outside, then turn off porch lights or landscape lighting to lessen light pollution.
- **Don't allow open access to garbage.** Secure trash cans and refuse areas to discourage animals like coyotes, foxes, bears, and rodents, who will quickly prefer human food over what they might normally eat in the wild. Human food sources draw them dangerously close to us, both in terms of proximity and habit.
- **Plant native species** to help birds and insects thrive. Research which species are local to your area; some insects depend on a narrow range of plants for their food. Assist pollinators by planting single-petalled cultivars and hybrids instead of complicated doubles, which can prevent access to nectar and pollen.
- **Cultivate an air of imperfection** in your garden and never resort to using synthetic pesticides and herbicides. The risks and destruction to the wider ecosystem far outweigh the benefits of solving a small horticultural problem.

OPPOSITE (*clockwise form top left*): Garden visitors include flower longhorn beetles, turkeys, butterflies, and bumblebees.

Pollinators come in many guises, including wasps.

A forest of self-sown fennel in the gravel garden.

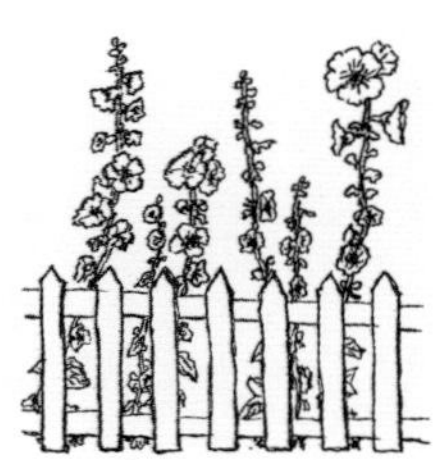

GARDEN GIANTS

I can't imagine having a garden that doesn't feature several tall plants that grow as spires. They offer an indispensable design element, functioning as exclamation points. By tall, I mean anywhere from four feet to a little more than six, or even higher for some varieties that can grow to eight feet. Because of their stature, these plants have a different character than those growing in loose, rounded shapes and offer much more immediate interest than a plant that grows so low you have to kneel down to admire it. Spire plants are fascinating to walk among. With their human scale, you can almost feel the life force of the plant as you walk through a group of them, as if they were a crowd of people. On some days, all I want to do is stare eye to eye with a hollyhock blossom.

When I worked as a garden editor at *Martha Stewart Living*, I did a photo shoot at Avena Botanicals, an herb garden in Maine owned by herbalist Deb Soule. One of this unique garden's most transporting moments is an area populated by one such "crowd" formed by tall Greek mullein (*Verbascum olympicum*), which is used in herbology as a respiratory aid. It has beautiful felted, silvery leaves and candle-like flower spikes dotted with butter yellow flowers. I made a mental note to plant something similar one day. Many spire plants are biennials, meaning they form a low rosette of leaves their first year and then shoot up to bloom in their second year, after which they expire, scattering seeds (often liberally) to start the process all over again. Some plants listed as biennials, like angelicas and certain verbascums, can also be short-lived perennials, depending on genetic variations and growing conditions. The differentiation can be confusing, once again proving that though we humans keep trying to classify nature into strict boxes, she still does what she wants, ignoring our attempts at categorization.

Currently I have several verbascums in my garden—mainly the shorter purple mulleins (*V. phoeniceum*) with their beautiful dusky colors in a range of plum, copper, rust, and peach—and the nettle-leaved mullein hybrids of *V. chaixii*. As we develop the gravel garden, I want to include many more of the larger types, which can reach up to ten feet high, such as the common mullein (*V. thapsus*) or the giant silver mullein (*V. bombyciferum*), so I can have my own verbascum party to walk through.

When we had our garden in upstate New York, foxgloves were one of the few plants we could grow that the deer didn't ravage. There's something magical about these flowers; they belong in a children's storybook. I love the way the bell-shaped blossoms dangle on the stalk, graduating from larger to smaller as they climb up. Bees relish them too, as they clamber drunkenly into the blossoms and disappear for several seconds. Then, just when you think they aren't coming out, they start scooting backward with their furry butts and legs covered in pollen. As well as being a magnet for pollinators, foxgloves also attract stories and folklore. Their common name has many proposed origins, but my favorite is that the word "fox" is a derivation of "folks," a nickname for the evil faeries of European folklore. These aren't the cute Tinkerbell fairies, but the malevolent, vengeful creatures that can be guilty of kidnapping and vandalism. In some stories, they are supposed to wear the tubular flowers on their fingers as folk's-gloves. Keeping with the finger idea, the botanical genus name of *Digitalis* comes in. Because the plant acts on the heart, its power was once harnessed to make the heart medicine of the same name, but its effective dose range is very narrow, and it can just as easily cause heart failure. That feature, along with the dark red blots that line the throat of many varieties, give it the other old names of bluidy man's fingers or dead-men's bells. If you see a foxglove blossom moving slightly without the presence of breeze or bee, maybe one of the folks is hiding in there ready to cause some malfeasance.

Most foxgloves are biennials, and though I've bought a full-grown ready-to-bloom plant a few times, I've been growing them successfully from seed for more than twenty years. Our usual technique is to sow them wherever we think they might grow. In the upstate garden, they flourished in a woodland setting, moist with fallen leaves and underbrush. They seemed to enjoy the shade from the high canopy of hemlocks and beeches. I wasn't sure if they would like our sunnier, sandy situation on the Outer Cape but it turns out they love it here too. I usually sow the seeds in late June, around the same time the blossoms naturally fade and scatter theirs. As biennials, they make a rosette of leaves the first year and then bloom the next before dying. They self-seed very effectively each year, so you'll have a constant supply. The most common foxglove is the plain pink *Digitalis purpurea* but there are many related hybrids in a range of colors. 'Pam's Choice' is white with dark red splotches in the throat. 'Dalmation Peach', 'Sutton's Apricot', and 'Camelot Cream' come in the warmer shades their names indicate. The yellow perennial foxglove (*D. grandiflora*) has been in several of my gardens, and it is longer-lived and the toughest I've grown. I've tried some of the other more unusual species such as the rusty foxglove (*D. ferruginea*), the Grecian or woolly foxglove (*D. lanata*), and the chocolate foxglove (*D. parviflora*), which feature enviable shades of bronze, rust, or brown. I desire them most—because I've never been able to get them to bloom. This year I'm getting more serious about my efforts. Instead of direct-seeding in the garden, I'm going to start the seeds indoors in pots so they'll be stronger when I plant them out.

Hollyhocks have always been a goal of mine. They wouldn't grow in any of my gardens before. At six to eight feet, they were too tall for our windy Chelsea rooftop. The upstate cabin and Des Moines locations were both too humid (hollyhocks are prone to rust, a disfiguring fungus, when overly wet). Here are on the Cape they've done quite well, both from direct-sown seed and when put in the border as small plants. They come in a pastel rainbow of colors, but two of my favorites are the near-black 'Nigra' and the butter yellow 'Rugose'; the latter is supposed to be rust-resistant. Fingers crossed the fungus won't show up here because it's so hard to get rid of that many people swear off hollyhocks. This year I'm trying 'Crème de Cassis', with its white flowers and black currant-stained throats, for the first time. I haven't grown any of the many double hybrids, partly because I think they look so overbred, but also because the doubling up of the petals makes it harder for pollinators to access the nectar and pollen.

The queen of the spire plants must be the stately delphinium. So tall, so vividly blue, so finicky, this perennial inspires its devotees, though you don't see many gardeners going to the trouble of planting the classic tall varieties. They are one of those aspirational plants that are hard to grow in most parts of our country, though they can do well in the Pacific Northwest and the northern parts of New England and Canada. One summer, we had the good fortune to be taken by a friend to see Jardin Les Quatre Vents, a large private estate garden in Quebec. There was much to marvel at throughout the twenty-acre garden, but the plants I recall most vividly were the giant delphiniums that were incredibly tall and full-flowered. They love rich, fertile soil, so the gardener must have grown them in well-manured beds because they towered above my head in ultraviolet shades ranging from pale blue to electric indigo to deepest purple to white and pink. I don't think I can match that here on Cape Cod, but I'm going to try some of the shorter types like 'Heirloom Blue Mirror' and 'Magic Fountains Mix', which seem to be easier to figure out. I do, however, have great luck with larkspurs, their annual relatives. Though not as tall, they have an airy grace and a similar color range. Last year, I had a banner year with the plants growing to about four feet tall.

Some other spires aren't biennials so they're a little easier to deal with because they don't need replanting as often. Like delphiniums, monkshood come in a rich purplish-blue that's a rarity in the garden, and they bloom late, until October. The hooded flowers look sinister, and they are, being poisonous even to the touch and even more deadly if ingested. This was the plant favored by the court poisoners of Imperial Rome, who were often women because they had access to the cooking pot. Not dangerous at all, culver's root (*Veronicastrum virginicum*) is one of the most graceful plants with its candle-like spires made up of tiny white flowers. It gives a less showy, but elegant rhythm to a flower bed. Other towering plants in my garden that aren't as spire-like include our native great burnet (*Sanguisorba officinalis* 'Red Thunder'), which grows to about six feet or more. Its delicate tracery of garnet-colored thimbles dance on wiry, curving stems, while American burnet (*S. canadensis*) is covered with dangling fuzzy white flowers that resemble feathers. It was new to me this past summer and quickly reached seven feet. Nursery listings say it likes being in moist soil near a wetland but both plants thrived last summer during a drought.

If they are wispy enough, taller varieties add an unexpected note when planted sporadically at the front of the flower border as see-through plants. I'm thinking here of the beloved annual *Verbena bonariensis* that produces purple flowers sitting high on top of wiry stems. It's an easy, indispensable plant and I put it everywhere. Similarly, I've begun adding more tall snapdragons like those from the 'Rocket' series, which when staked can grow to four feet tall and have been living through the winter in my climate. Until now, I had no idea that snapdragons were anything more than annuals. Also, for the front of the border but still spire-y, I've recently come to plant the bottlebrush-looking blazing star, especially the white variety (*Liatris spicata* 'Floristan White'). Taller native types, like meadow blazing star (*L. ligulistylis*) and rough blazing star (*L. aspera*), have flower stems with punctuated clusters of purple flowers that look more graceful than the common purple *L. spicata* that is so tightly packed.

From the world of bulbs, I had great luck last year with 'Summer Drummer' allium, which bloomed with purple flowers on sturdy brownish-purple stems more than five feet tall. I was surprised how well it held up to our maritime winds and drought. The seedheads lasted well into winter, and the rhythm of their spherical heads in the long border was probably the only design feature that actually worked over those months. This year, I planted another holy grail plant I've never had luck with, foxtail lilies (*Eremurus*), which sport bottlebrush spires that can reach eight feet in height and bloom in warm pastels of pale oranges, yellows, and whites. Success! As I write this, they are about four feet tall and in bud but stretching to their ultimate height.

Most of these plants need staking of some sort. Last summer was so busy, garden maintenance took a backseat to life. As a result, I barely added supports to anything. By fall, plants were tilting, looking a little cockeyed, and in need of attention. Another consideration for spire plants are their feet and ankles. Some of them have attractive mounds of leaves at the base, but others, like the alliums, have unsightly yellowing leaves that take away from the beautiful flowers above. Plant low, mounding perennials, such as hardy geraniums or salvias, in front of the spire plants to hide anything you don't want to see so as not to distract from the glories above.

OPPOSITE (*clockwise from top left*): A garden gate is obscured by tall ironweed and white sanguisorba; 'Rugose' hollyhocks; foxtail lilies; 'Dalmatian Peach' foxgloves.

LESSON

PERENNIAL-STAKING STRATEGIES

I am a lazy staker with my perennials, so most of these tips fall under the category of "Take my advice; I'm not using it." However, I am trying to be better. Here are some techniques I'm trying to use to achieve my goal of having my staking be as unobtrusive and natural-looking as possible.

• **Secure single stakes early.** For tall single-stemmed plants like hollyhocks, delphiniums, and dahlias, secure pole stakes with soft materials that won't cut or bind the stems, including soft garden ties, twine, or strips of fabric that might blend in. Wrap the stem and support in a figure eight pattern for added security. Install the stakes as early as possible and avoid stabbing the root ball. If you have prevailing winds, angle or position the stake so that it is supporting the plant against the wind's direction. I use natural materials, such as bamboo or wood, instead of plastic, and check growth progress regularly.

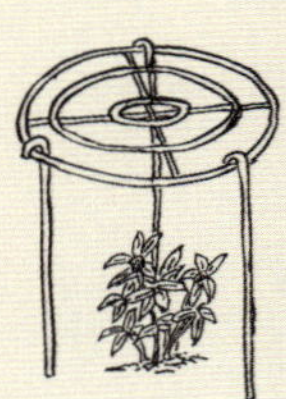

• **Stop flopping or splitting with ring, grid, or hoop supports.** Peonies, asters, phlox, rudbeckias, chrysanthemums, and any perennials prone to flopping or splitting due to their heavy flowers or from rainstorms benefit from these metal (usually green or black) gridded hoops supported on legs. These manufactured off-the-shelf supports come in a range of shapes and sizes. They must be installed early so that the plant grows through them. Trying to shove the support over the fully grown foliage will only make the plant look misshapen or will damage it. I rarely use these because I find the green metal cages overly conspicuous before the plants have grown in.

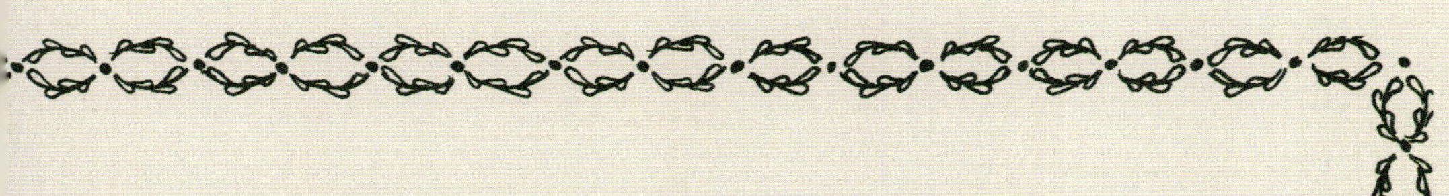

•**Support with pea sticks.** As an alternative to the above, I try to support my blooming perennials with pea sticks or brush gathered from around the garden. I like these natural supports because they tend to disappear among the plants while their branches help multi-stemmed perennials stay upright. You can use pliable branches to make basketweave twig domes that will do the same job as the hoop supports but with a more natural appearance.

• **Depending on your preference, try tomato cages.** Some gardeners successfully use these sturdy metal cages for taller plants like asters or heleniums. I find them generally too restrictive and visually obtrusive, but my friend Frances Palmer uses them for her dahlia garden. Once the plants are full-grown, they are barely noticeable so I might give them another try in a big flower border.

An October flower harvest of dahlias, hardy mums, salvia, and hardy geraniums.

JUST A SNIP

Though I've been drawn to all things floral since a young age, I did not grow up in a home that had fresh cut flowers around the house. When I was very small, I remember several arrangements of plastic flowers that were dotted around as décor, particularly one of blue roses that I found oddly intriguing. Later, we graduated to silk when that became fashionable. I much preferred the upgrade because they looked more realistic, so I would spend my allowance money by walking over to the nearby Gibson's Discount Center and buying my own supply of flowers to play with. Evidently, I had a flair for it. My mom liked my creations enough to pay me a little extra allowance periodically to redo the arrangements so that they looked better. I'd then use the money to go buy more silk flowers in a kind of floral economic loop. As my parents dubbed me at the time, I was a true "flower child"—whether the flowers were real or fake didn't matter. Now that I'm a gardener, I want the real thing—especially in the winter, when I always have something blooming in the house to combat the winter doldrums: a potted amaryllis or paperwhites, cut tulips or fragrant lilies from the corner florist. Now I am lucky enough to live in a house with fresh flowers available for cutting nine months of the year—during the other three I make do pretty well from the grocery store.

I've visited other people's gardens and admired how they designed cutting gardens so that they don't have to deplete their flower beds. Until we got to the Cape, I never had a big enough yard to even think about such a designated area. Though we have more space now, for some reason, the concept of devoting beds just to grow flowers for cutting feels like a waste of space. In my former gardens, I always planted flowers for cutting but without setting them apart. I incorporated them into my regular planting beds and containers even though there wasn't much space. In most growing seasons there were enough blooms to arrange for the dinner table when guests came over. I've taken the same approach in my new garden.

I try to have an almost year-round plan—a calendar of flowers. In the spring, I cut wave after wave of bulb flowers: from winter aconites and snowdrops to daffodils, anemones, and hyacinths that begin in March and April. Tulips round out the early show in time for the lilacs to bloom in May. I usually don't mix the lilacs with anything; a big vase of them is so luxurious on their own. For me, poppies and other annuals are always the stars in a bouquet, but I also add herbs: leaves of rosemary, sage, fennel, dill (I love the pungent scent of dill mixed with the sweetness of roses), basil (especially the purple varieties), anise hyssop, and marjoram. Silver leaves from lavender, curry plant, and dusty miller make a neutral base and work with any flower color.

Later in the season, summer bulbs, like dahlias, bearded irises, and lilies, come into their own. As with the lilacs, I don't usually mix the lilies with anything else. They're structurally so dramatic with their rod-like stems and dangling lantern flowers—any other blossom would just get in their way. Sometimes I grab as many dahlias as I can without robbing the beds of flowers and put them in one big vase; other times I like to mix them with daintier flowers or grass seedheads to soften their sturdy vegetal nature. Speaking of grasses, picking wild plants from the edges of the property or even the roadside gives an arrangement a rough element that I like. But I take only imported invasives like white campion or honesty from the wild and leave the valuable native regional flora alone. In the spring, I might add dangling white racemes of local black cherry; in the fall, some oak or beech leaves. Over the winter, a few judicious snips of bayberry, juniper, or winterberry branches bring the beauty of the nearby woods inside, while adding strong plant supports for weaker-stemmed flowers.

In the raised vegetable beds, I sow balsam impatiens, calendula, nigella, poppies, and violas both for pollinators but also to add to arrangements. I also include edible flowers, such as nasturtiums, and the umbel flowers of basil, chervil, dill, and parsley. In the long border, I scatter hardy annuals like poppies and cornflowers early in the summer followed by dahlias and tall shrubby salvias, such as burgundy 'Van Houttei', deep blue-purple 'Amistad', and pale blue *Salvia azurea.* In the herb garden, a mix of culinary and historic herbs work well in a vase as do anemones, more calendulas, hellebores, roses, and yarrow. In the gravel garden, bearded irises will have their brief but glorious moment as will flowering oregano, santolina, fennel, and a dozen types of lavender. Any of these blossoms can be clipped without causing much visual impact to the overall garden.

I prefer having all the floral material I use for bouquets to live in fellowship with other plants in the garden beds. If I had a separate place to harvest them, there would be gaps every time I took too many and the next round would take weeks, if not months, to fill back in. In this plan, my cuts are almost imperceptible to the grander visual scheme. None of my beds are intended solely for cutting per se, yet at the same time my whole garden is designed for harvesting flowers. There will always be certain blooms that I want to view and study more closely indoors. Placing flowers in a vase on a table or mantel sets them apart, abstracting them from their natural setting to help us see their intrinsic beauty, the subtlest of which might be easy to miss out in the yard.

OVERLEAF, LEFT (*clockwise from top left*): Martagon lilies; December berries and evergreens; hyacinths in a tiered vase; apple blossoms.

OVERLEAF, RIGHT: A tone-on-tone arrangement of reddish-black tulips and hellebores.

WHEN WE LOST THE BIG TREE

We weren't at the house the day the giant silver maple came down. It was during a rare early nor'easter that arrived on Halloween. We had just moved in the previous spring and were getting to know our new home. The ninety-by-ninety-foot maple was definitely the most distinctive aspect of our property and was a landmark tree in the neighborhood, towering over our small Cape Cod–style house. I loved the way it framed the simplicity of the façade, which is basically what any preschooler might draw to represent a house. A central door, flanked by two windows on each side, all secured by a brick chimney to withstand storms and hurricanes.

Our tree, however, wasn't so lucky. Just a few months earlier, my knowledgeable gardening friend Susan had visited and, seeing the imposing specimen, asked, "Is that a silver maple? Be careful. They are notoriously short-lived and shallow rooted." Not three months later, the tree was down—the victim of the early nor'easter whose high winds struck the 116-year-old tree while it was still in full leaf, knocking it over like a capsized sailboat. It was an unlucky break so early in our homeownership. But we, and our neighbors across the street whose 250-year-old Siberian elm snapped in half during the same storm, were actually lucky—neither tree hit our houses. The neighbor's elm had been there since the time of the sea captain who built the house. It had watched the Outer Cape go from whaling to cod fishing to the formation of an art colony, and then tourism. The tree would have been captured forever by Edward Hopper in a 1930 painting titled

Rich's House, except that he decided to edit it out of his artwork to show more of the building.

Our tree was less storied, but still I was calmed by its cool, leafy presence. Silver maples are native to the eastern United Sates so it's impossible to know if it was planted by someone, but it was there before our house was moved to its present location in the 1930s. It laid down gracefully in the backyard, its massive four-foot-diameter trunk leaning completely over while the tips of the branches grazed the house gutters, denting only one. It did smash two privet hedges (now grown back) and helpfully crumpled an ugly cyclone fence that was going to be removed anyway. Our neighbor came to check on it after the storm and called us with what she worried was terrible news. After a momentary shock, I rolled right into the positive aspects of the accident. Clearly it was a dangerous tree to have been planted so close to the house. If the wind, which neighbors thought might be classed as a microburst from the sandy cliffs of the open Atlantic nearby, had blown at a different angle, it would've crushed our house and all its history.

The other plus was our new accessibility to the sun. The tree's canopy was huge and dense and covered the area that we wanted for our raised-bed vegetable garden. When I first saw the place in March, I had hoped there might be enough sun for tomatoes, herbs, and salad greens. By the time the tree leafed out, I realized that wouldn't work. Now that the tree is gone, I have all the sun I need in that space, and enough area on either side of the hedge to put in some perennial borders. None of this would've happened under the maple, whose extensive root system made digging a real chore. Within a few years, the tree roots had decomposed, making digging through and around them much easier. The biodegraded matter from the former tree also enriched our sandy soil, making other growth possible. Silver maples (*Acer saccharinum*) are somewhat allelopathic, meaning they put out chemicals in the soil to inhibit the growth of nearby plants. I don't know if the chemicals dissipate once the tree dies, but I haven't noticed any negative effects from the leftover tree roots.

Our tree was not one of the so-called wolf trees—those stragglers left behind by early European settlers after they had cut down most of the trees or let their animals graze out the saplings that stood on the land. Ours may have been newer, but still, longtimers told us our maple was one of the largest in the area. Colonists overharvested most all the old growth for timber. If you see photographs or paintings of the area from a hundred years ago or so, you'll notice an almost treeless moonscape of rolling heathland and farm fields. It was a reductive landscape that Hopper and other Cape Cod artists loved to paint. Now the area is much more forested, dense with a combination of pitch pine, black oak, and white oak. But large non-native trees like our former specimen are rare. On our property we also have black locusts, red maples, and beeches, the latter of which are struggling with beech leaf disease.

Establishing new trees is a challenge. Along with powerful storms, we have sandy soil that doesn't give roots much foundation or nutrition. We later found out one reason our maple was so large was that it had tapped into the old septic system, which had to be replaced by the previous owner before the house was sold to us. The excavators told us that there was heavy root infestation and even a small maple growing in the tank. It seems that clever silver maples are famous for accessing sewer lines for their own benefit. After losing the tree, we wanted to plant another one quickly, farther away from the house. So, we planted three European hornbeams, which are supposed to be relatively fast-growing but also strong and wind resistant. Usually, the faster a tree grows, the weaker its wood. The hornbeams haven't taken off as much as I'd like. Maybe it's a lack of water or nutrients, but I hope they will reach their third-year "leap" in the "sleep-creep-leap" cycle soon.

Losing our maple tree taught me to shift gears when the unexpected does sneak up on you and to look for the positive outcomes wherever possible. We can't fight nature, nor should we try. I'm sure this is not the last storm-related damage we'll be dealing with, even though our house is fairly sheltered. Now, I'm just waiting for the replacement hornbeams to start looking more like real trees instead of saplings. It's not easy to be patient when it comes to trees—but that in itself is a life lesson worth living during an age where the immediate-delivery sense of gratification tops everything else.

The silver maple once dwarfed our antique Cape Cod house, which was relocated here from a neighboring town in the 1930s.

LET SLEEPING LEAVES LIE

I'm an advocate for not cleaning up garden beds in fall and winter. Allowing everything to collapse into the earth after the first hard frost feels right. I leave the twigs, leaves, and branches primarily to support overwintering wildlife, but also, a garden filled with plants, even if they're dormant, is more interesting to look at in winter than a garden that's been cut back and swept bare. This is not a revolutionary position. The practice has been increasingly recognized within horticultural circles over the past decades as a good way to support ecological balance and biodiversity. In addition, at the end of a busy season of gardening, I don't feel like doing the hard work of tidying everything up.

Lazy gardeners like me have Dutch landscape designer Piet Oudolf and other practitioners of the natural garden style to thank for giving us the permission to forgo a late fall cleanup. Previously, the common horticultural practice was to rake up any leaves or plant litter in the planting beds because the debris could harbor diseases over the winter and return with a vengeance the following spring and summer. Oudolf is as much a visual artist as he is a creator of high-profile landscapes like the High Line in New York City and Lurie Garden in Millennium Park in Chicago. In the process, he made dormant (non-gardeners would say "dead") plants fashionable. He promotes perennials, many of them North American natives, for the late-stage beauty and stark architecture they give to a garden from fall through winter and into the spring cutback that occurs as the new growth begins.

As I write this, it's a few days before New Year's Eve and we've already had temperatures in the mid-teens and a decent snowstorm where the snow stuck for a few days. Generally, if you live in a part of the country that historically had more snow before climate change, your plants are missing the comforting blanket of insulation that a deep winterlong snow provides from wind and temperature fluctuations. The frozen moisture is valuable as a natural drip irrigation for plants over a long period, with a big release of water when temperatures warm in spring just as plants and animals emerge and need it the most. The snow drought is real. Mud season, that period of melt in the northern states just after a prolonged snow cover or "snowpack," used to be in late spring but now stretches over most of the winter months. According to a study in the journal *Nature*, snowpack in the continental United States has shrunk 10 to 20 percent per decade over the last forty years, especially in the Southwestern and Northeastern United States. If you are of a certain age and think you are seeing less snow than you did when you were a child—you are.

Today, after a rare overnight snowstorm, I look out at a bright four to five inches of snow. The dark graphic lines of dormant plant stalks, half-hidden leaves, and seedheads stand in stark profile against the almost blinding whiteness. But within this graphic landscape all sorts of pollinators are at work building nests in the stems during winter and early spring. Native bees set up in dried stems with each larva sealed in its cell alongside a bundle of pollen as a food source. Other insects also look for hollow or pithy stems, such as thistles, raspberries, yuccas, or bee balms. You can help them along in the early spring by creating nest cavities by cutting your dead stems back to eighteen to twenty-four inches. As the summer progresses, new growth will cover the older stems with the larvae inside. They will overwinter in the previous year's stems and then emerge and fly off the following spring. We need to leave these shorter stems up much longer than just one winter. Often, you can tell if insects are nesting in your stems when you see the ends sealed up with mud or debris.

Out in the long border, several tall native ironweeds (*Vernonia noveboracensis*) tower unstaked at eight feet. Already the survivors of several big storms, they are regularly visited by cardinals and groups of Carolina wrens. Flanking them are a couple of burnets (*Sanguisorba officinalis*), which, though looking a bit squishy, are still standing tall. There are the wispy, goose-down remnants of milkweed pods, several gothic spires of culver's root (*Veronicastrum virginicum*), the button-headed seedheads of wild bergamot (*Monarda fistulosa*), and pincushions of mountain mint in a range of colors from gold to mahogany to coal black. The tiered seed compartments of Jerusalem sage (*Phlomis fruticosa*) always elicit a "What is that?" from visitors. A tall, red-twigged spray of smooth blue aster (*Symphyotrichum laeve* 'Bluebird') is an astonishment; covered with the stars of its spent flower heads it still stands about four feet high after bursting forth in a delicate cloud of pale lilac flowers in September.

Interspersed among the brown, signs of life remain. Last summer's tall snapdragons, now fallen over but retaining their leaves, snake dark green through the underbrush like their namesakes. The serrated leaves of the silvery cardoon mingle during the off-season with the jade-colored foliage of the alliums. Their starry, spherical seedheads would still be standing if I hadn't cut them earlier to bring inside for a dried arrangement. This year's foxglove leaves and the wilted swords of the bearded irises wait for the coming warmth so they can produce next summer's flowers. Nearby, the rhododendron leaves furl dramatically every time the temperature goes well below freezing, creating a useful visual thermometer as I look out the window.

In the gravel garden, dark seedheads of the taller sedums are still erect and one plant looks particularly showy in a trio with a Spanish lavender and a shrubby caryopteris covered in spent blossoms. Ferns of little fennel seedlings nap at the bottom of last year's stalks that once reached eight feet in height. A hoist of silvery plants still hold court in the front herb garden. The artemisia clan—southernwood, mugwort, wormwood, and the hybrids 'Silver Mound' and 'Valerie Finnis'—still look fresh, though maybe a little bedraggled on the bottom parts of the stems. The silver curry plant (*Helichrysum angustifolium*), often sold as an annual north of Zone 8, is still standing here in our Zone 7B sandy soil. As are the various hellebores, germander, lavenders, marjoram, and thyme. I have a fond spot in my garden for hellebores; they are one of my best performing plants because they have something to offer all year. The older leaves may look a little tired, but I can already see the first pinkish-white flower buds emerging from the Christmas rose hybrids of *Helleborus niger.* Though they are native to the high Alps, they seem to be quite happy here near the beach. Soon all the various shades of Lenten roses (*H. orientalis*) will join them in early spring

My raised beds out back are not as picturesque. They would not look out of place at an abandoned homestead. Being either busy or lazy—I can't remember which—I cleaned them up minimally at the end of the season by taking down the twig teepees that once supported peas, pole beans, and then tomatoes. After the snow melted, it's still a pretty lively mess when I peer more closely. Rooting around, I find a handful of squat 'Royal Chantenay' carrots (someone had nibbled off their green leaves but left the roots behind). And I know there are still some overlooked potatoes lurking as are some baby radishes and Asian greens left over from one last October seeding. They made it through the teen temps and I'm eager to see if they last through the January, February, March, March, March of our long Cape springs, taking off when things get warmer. Shallot and garlic bulbs are sending up green shoots. A giant stand of parsley wilts when it's below freezing but bounces back. Chervil overwinters as a low rosette of leaves next to thyme and marjoram. A big sturdy sage looks ready to last for months. And everywhere, I see signs of plants germinating even here on December 29: poppies, larkspurs, and others too tiny to identify. I'm happy to see that here, so soon after the solstice, the rhythm of life has turned its self-appointed corner, and new life is taking shape and putting down root even though months of winter lie ahead of us.

Silhouettes of ironweed seedheads.

OVERLEAF, LEFT (*clockwise from top left*): Aster seedheads; tomatillo husks; milkweed pods; the snow arrives but never stays long these days.

OVERLEAF, RIGHT: Hardy salad greens still lurk under the first snows.

REJUVENATION

I woke up on a beautiful mid-November day. The sun was blissfully strong. The sky was almost the exact color of the spring flowers that would later emerge from the squill bulbs I planned to plant that day. But I was feeling at loose ends. So much change was happening around me—a career shift, politics, the power struggles of the global world order. The main emotion I felt was unease.

Years ago, a yoga teacher told me "Stress comes from trying to control the uncontrollable." Those big moving targets weren't going to be corralled by me on that beautiful day. I think of those words from time to time, including that November morning. So, I decided to heed her call and take charge of something I could control.

I had a neglected garden bed in mind. About twelve-by-sixteen feet, it sits right outside our back door and has been a problematic planting area since we bought the Cape house. It was packed with a dense carpet of lily of the valley that must have been first planted many decades ago. The first spring they emerged I was transported by the heady scent that wafted into the window before I even knew they were out there. It is one of my favorite flower fragrances—carrying both green notes and white notes at the same time. As anyone who has grown lily of the valley knows, they are rampant spreaders with aggressive roots. I could barely get my shovel in, even with a fully weighted shove of my foot. Over the next couple of seasons, I found a few spots I could cram in some plants: a 'Korean Spice' viburnum (*Viburnum carlesii*), Oriental lilies, a white mallow, some columbines, and lungworts. But nothing ever really thrived. They were strangled by the lily of the valley and a tenacious weedy grass with aggressive runners that crept in whenever I turned around.

Standing with my shovel and looking at the mass of brown weedy leaves, I decided to take control by dismantling the bed and putting it back together again. It was something I'd never done on such a scale before and I was winging it. I worked in chunks, each one a shovel deep and about a foot square, almost like cubed brownie slices of soil topped with matted roots. I sliced ten or so of the pieces in advance and then got on my hands and knees, picked up a brownie, knocked the soil off (thankfully it had been dry weather followed by light rain), and pulled the lily of the valley roots and grass runners away from any valuable perennials or bulbs I wanted to keep. In a few hours, I was about halfway through the bed and surrounded by piles of plant material. I extracted the lily of the valley roots due to be replanted. Blond and soilless, they looked almost like excelsior packing material. The grass runners I put in a throwaway pile. The keeper plants went into a box for a few hours until I could replant them. A couple of friends stopped by to say hello in the middle of my labors and they found me covered in dirt, but with a big smile on my face.

For two afternoons, I dug and sifted on my hands and knees. It felt so satisfying. Square foot by square foot, I was taking charge of what had once been a beautiful spot for the woman who originally owned the house and reclaiming it. I imagined her planting the lilies of the valley in the 1930s when the house was moved here from nearby Wellfleet. I pictured her putting in the pips with the hope that one day they'd be rewarded with a fragrant sea of flowers. If she could see them now, I trust she'd be happy I was rescuing the plants set in place all those years ago. For as rampant and competitive as those lilies of the valley are, I love them; I just didn't want them there. I replanted them in an area at the back of the garden, under two tall junipers, where I hoped they will be as successful as they were before.

Once done, I had a cleared garden bed I could use. After returning the plants I extracted to their rightful places, I added the recent shipment of bulbs. The soil was so loose and friable I didn't even have to use a trowel. I could dig the bulbs in as deeply as needed with my gloved hands. Crocuses, snowdrops, and rock garden irises were up toward the front of the bed near the walkway where I could easily see them, come March and April. Daffodils, of course, mainly white. More Oriental and Chinese trumpet lilies as well as martagons. Dutch irises, something new for me. And later, next spring, I'll fold in some more part-shade perennials, such as sweet woodruff and lungworts.

While I worked, I listened to the audiobook version of *Circe* by Madeline Miller. It's the *Odyssey* told from the perspective of the enchantress/goddess Circe herself. I listened to the vivid descriptions of her digging around in the earth for powerful herbs on Aiaia, the island where she was exiled by the Olympians. In the book, Miller vividly writes about the smell of the damp earth and the pungency of the growing herbs and Circe's sense of isolation and her resilience in exile. I could smell similar evocative scents as I worked. Next spring, when the flower bed bursts into bloom, I know I'll remember very fondly those November days when rejuvenating a neglected garden bed rejuvenated me as well.

OVERLEAF, LEFT: Personal goal: a cleared planting bed.

OVERLEAF, RIGHT: The entangled roots of a long-established lily of the valley planting.

LESSON

TRANSPLANTING TIPS

Good transplanting practices are not only an essential part of having a successful and healthy garden; they are also a good way to save money as you reposition or divide established perennials. Here are some suggestions for doing it safely and effectively.

- Transplant when the surrounding soil is moist but not too dry or too wet. If rain has been scarce, irrigate the bed around the potential transplants the day before.
- Have your new planting hole ready so that the transplant is not sitting in the open air or sun with its roots exposed. If you do need to keep them out, place a wet cloth over them so they don't dry out.
- Make the new hole slightly larger than the root ball. Add some new soil to the hole or compost around the top after you've planted it. Water the plant in thoroughly, giving it a slow soaking that reaches the roots.
- Only use well-aged compost or manure around new plantings. And underdo rather than overdo any soil amendments until the plant's roots are settled in and growing.
- Don't be overly rough with the exposed roots, but it is good to tickle them apart if they seem root-bound or if you are pulling a new plant out of a root-bound pot.
- Generally, match the soil level of the plant from the old location to the new. Make sure it doesn't sit so high that all the water runs away from the plant. I like to make a little dike of soil around the root ball to capture irrigation and rainfall.
- Mulch around the transplant, avoiding the crown and keep your eye on it for several days to make sure it isn't wilting or in need of water.

A LITTLE NIGHT GARDENING

Coming home from work on a hot summer day, I immediately take off my shoes, put on shorts, and head out on the roof to water the garden. As the sun sets on the far side of the Hudson River, I go from pot to pot, filling each with the hose. As I splash around, I can't resist the urge to lean down and inhale from each night-scented flower I pass. The scents are hard to describe but generally they smell extraordinarily foreign—the opposite of everyday city smells like car exhaust, asphalt, and summer garbage. These are tropical perfumes, sometimes overpowering, sometimes only caught when my nose is right in the source, or sometimes they seem ineffable, lifted up in a breeze from some unknown bloom.

This scene is from a roof garden I left behind a long time ago, the first garden we made on a Chelsea rooftop in the 1990s. I don't recall exactly why I started to focus on plants that come into their own in the evening. But it makes sense, seeing how I never made it home from my job until well after six and I generally wanted to get right outside and enjoy the garden. I quicky realized that white or light-colored flowers catch the moonlight but also the lights from the surrounding buildings in a way that gives outdoor spaces a visual boost after dark. Several books about nocturnal gardening and fragrant flowers inspired me in my early life as an urban gardener. Peter Loewer's *The Evening Garden: Flowers and Fragrance from Dusk Till Dawn* (1993) introduced me to the concept and the plants. I studied classics like *The Fragrant Path* (1932) by Louise Beebe Wilder for more plants to grow from her descriptive entries on night-scented flowers. Of course, I realize that the light-catching colors and evening scents of these flowers are not here to please me but to lure pollinators like moths, bats, and beetles. Unless you're in the middle of a city like I was, evening gardens should be dark when you're not enjoying them, dependent only on moonlight versus landscape lighting or porch lights if possible. Turn off outside lights when they aren't in use so that they don't interfere with nocturnal pollinators who find the multiple light sources confusing for their navigation. Unlike flowers that close at sunset (a phenomenon called floral nyctinasty), night-blooming or night-fragrant plants open, or release their scent, to attract a different group of nocturnal pollinators who are drawn to the pale colors and floral fragrances that lure them to the nectar source.

I saw hawkmoths most frequently, but still, they startled me, flitting by suddenly to hover at the open throat of a datura or moonflower. The first time one appeared, I thought it was a nocturnal hummingbird. I had been previously unaware that tomato and tobacco hornworms are the caterpillar stage of the hawkmoth. If you see their large, fat bodies munching down your tomatoes, exercise caution before you kill them. The moths' fuzzy thoraxes transport pollen very effectively from flower to flower.

I revel in the heavy fragrances of these plants (though most of them don't open only at night like moonflowers, which will unfurl in front of your eyes at sunset). For a year or two, I had a small pot of spicy-scented Sambac or Arabian jasmine (*Jasminum sambac*) that I kept alive by overwintering indoors. An angel's trumpet (*Brugmansia suaveolens*) that scented the air with an almost soap-like perfume suffered the same way. I grew several types of devil's trumpets (*Datura*), which, though similar in flower shape to the angel's trumpets, aim upward instead of dangling down on their stems. Both have a similarly transporting scent and both are highly poisonous and hallucinogenic, which adds to their mystery. Moonflowers are one of the most visually impressive annual vines and are much better behaved than their self-seeding relatives, morning glories. Their pure white, crisply pleated blossoms resemble in look and size a dessert paper plate and catch the moonlight like a reflector. The only downside is that they take forever to bloom in the Northeast, so I start them as early as possible inside; otherwise, they don't flower until September.

Certain types of passionflowers, another subtropical vine, give off a fruity, bubblegum type of fragrance but the intensity tends to vary from hybrid to hybrid. I grew 'Incense' but there are other scented varieties, such as 'Inspiration' or our native fruit-producing maypop (*Passiflora incarnata*), the latter of which is hardy into New England. Another subtropical vining plant, night-blooming jessamine (*Cestrum nocturnum*), is one of the most intensely fragrant tropicals I've grown. We planted one from a small pot that grew to about three feet in one summer. The scent, which is released from pale green trumpets only at dusk, has an almost overwhelming candy smell, like SweeTARTS, but with a powdery effect that tickles your nose. In full bloom, it was so strong we often had to shut our bedroom window, which looked out over the rooftop terrace, so we could sleep. I tried it last summer on Cape Cod, but it didn't bloom as much as it did in the summer heat of New York City.

Some of my most beloved nighttime scents are from annuals. Like most of their class, they bloom generously and they're not generally difficult to grow. Mignonette (*Reseda odorata*) is an old-fashioned, inconsequential flower you wouldn't glance at during the day, but in the evening it fills the air with a particularly spicy, earthy smell with a violet top note that is hard to describe. Attributing scents is very personal, but its tiny flowers give off a fragrance that smells to me like Grey Flannel, an old Geoffrey Beene cologne I wore in high school and college in hopes that I would seem more grown-up and sophisticated. Old garden books tell several tales about mignonette (translated as "little darling"). Reported to have arrived in Europe when Napoleon sent seed to Josephine from Egypt, it was so widely grown as a window-box plant in nineteenth-century Paris that it perfumed the streets. I've tried two other scented annuals with varying success: night-scented stock (*Matthiola longipetala*) and night-blooming phlox (*Zaluzianskya capensis*). The first has the same distinctive spicy-sweet clove smell as common stock but blooms sparingly for me. Though

I've sown the latter multiple times, I have never had success getting it to bloom but, once again, I'll keep at it.

Flowering tobaccos (*Nicotiana*) are easy to grow from seed or from purchased nursery seedlings. Some of the shorter bedding types and the dramatic green *Nicotiana langsdorffii,* though useful for color, are unscented. Every year, I plant the tall woodland nicotiana (*N. sylvestris*) and the jasmine tobacco (*N. alata*), both for their glowing white trumpets and their tropical scents. Other common annuals, such as petunias, release their fragrances in the evening, though most hybrids are scentless. Look for smaller-flowered varieties that are less overbred and closer to the species, such as 'Balcony', 'Evening Scentsation', 'Old Fashioned Climbing', 'Rainmaster', and the double 'Tumbelina' series. Another plant with the 'Scentsation' hybrid name is verbena. Not the herb called lemon verbena, nor the tall border *Verbena bonariensis;* this is the old-fashioned bedding-out annual verbena. Many hybrids don't carry any scent, but the verbena 'Scentsation White' would be the ideal container plant for a moonlight garden. I've also found that some of the purple hybrids, such as 'Homestead Purple', carry an evening scent, but it can be hit or miss. Four o'clocks (*Mirabilis*), which I remember from my childhood, open and release their spicy fragrance in the late afternoon or evening, usually a little later than their named time. I grow the multi-colored mixes, though their vivid carnival shades can be challenging to put into a color scheme. The "Sweet-Scented Marvel of Peru" or *Mirabilis longiflora,* an heirloom plant that Thomas Jefferson grew at Monticello, is more demure. It releases its heavy scent from long white trumpets perfectly shaped for the tongue of a hawkmoth.

I first came across heliotrope (*Heliotropium arborescens*), a Victorian classic, as a relic from old gardening books. It seems to be more popular now at garden centers than when I first started gardening. One of its old common names, cherry pie, tells you something about its sweet scent, which doesn't exactly smell like cherries, though it has elements of almond and vanilla. Overall, it is a very powdery smell. The signature color of heliotrope is a glowingly deep purple, but white or pale lilac hybrids are commonly sold as well. Many of these plants we're calling annuals are tender perennials in their native habitat. And heliotropes, like datura, brugmansia, and cestrum, are toxic if ingested.

Because of the historic nature of my Cape Cod house, I've become interested in phlox more than ever before. For me, tall garden phlox (*Phlox paniculata*), is evocative of a grandmother's flower plot or a cottage garden. It has its detractors because of the tendency to mildew, but so far, mine has been very easy and accommodating, probably because of the good air circulation from the coastal breezes. To avoid getting mildew, keep the plants well-watered at ground level (but not on their leaves) and divide them every few years. The scent can surround you on a warm, still, humid night—a mix of jasmine and musky honey. There are many hybrids to choose from, but I usually veer away from the straight magenta varieties and head toward the blue or pale shades like the moonlight-white 'David', purple-blue 'Blue Paradise', or lilac and white 'Laura'. A new phlox I tried last year, 'Jeana', found growing wild in Tennessee a few years ago, has smaller flowers that are nearly magenta but with a bit more of a lilac-blue tone. It attracts lots of butterflies and, best of all, is resistant to mildew.

Fragrant summer bulbs can be planted after the frost date and still give you gusts of fragrance by midsummer. I've grown tuberoses in every garden I've had. They were formerly labeled *Polianthes tuberosa* but were recently recategorized as *Agave amica*. The classic type is the double Mexican tuberose 'The Pearl', which I grow, but I prefer the elegant single-flowered variety. I've also branched out into newer colored tuberoses in shades of yellow, pink, and light reddish-purple. The fragrant gladiola, also known as the peacock orchid or Abyssinian gladiola (*Gladiolus murielae*), is another night garden plant I make sure to include in my gardens. It couldn't be easier to grow, and its sword-like foliage makes a striking accent in pots even before it blooms. The flowers, which are white with a maroon throat, nod gracefully in the evening breeze as they release a fairly strong scent, which reminds me of the Coppertone suntan lotion of my youth. Another very fragrant and distinctive night-blooming bulb has many names, including ismene lily, Peruvian daffodil, and spider lily. Native to the Southern

United States and South America, its white or pale yellow flowers splay out like spider's legs. Its scent is heavy and tropical, especially on warm, humid evenings.

The reigning champions of evening fragrance are the garden lilies. The title "lily" has been given to almost any plant with a lily flower shape. Here, I'm only talking about members of the true lily genus, *Lilium.* Oriental and Trumpet classes can grow tall, often up to five feet, with large flowers that aim slightly downward and release an intoxicating fragrance. It can be suffocating to certain people, but I love it. Crosses between the two above classes produced the Orienpets. Due to their genetics, they are even larger and more floriferous. I don't usually grow the upward-facing Asiatic varieties because they seem less graceful, and their lack of fragrance is a real demerit. I always include the classic 'Regale', an heirloom lily native to China that was introduced to the United States in 1905. It has a pristine beauty, white with a wine-colored exterior, and a very strong scent. In the past few years, I've been having good luck with martagon lilies, which grow in an unusual, tiered fashion in warm shades of oranges, golds, and mauves. I always thought they'd be difficult because of the way people write about them, but here in my sandy soil with a bit of shade, they are flourishing. Don't let other people's cautionary tales keep you from experimenting.

Just as adding plant varieties that hit their peak in autumn expands your garden's potential past summer, nocturnal bloomers extend the garden till the wee hours. One of the things I enjoy most about having an evening-forward garden is that it's almost impossible to work in the garden after dark. So those chores and the to-do list that might distract you during the daytime evaporate into pure enjoyment when the sun goes below the horizon and the first, almost indecipherable, scent of an unfurling moonflower reaches your nose.

OPPOSITE (*clockwise from top left*): Orienpet lilies; flowering tobacco; blue flowers glow in the twilight; strongly scented night-blooming cestrum.

GOING SYMPHONIC

To refer to a feature in my garden as "The Long Border" sounds pretty grand, but it's not really. The main reason we created one was to solve a spatial problem that we encountered after our giant maple had been knocked over the previous fall. One day in the spring of 2022, I looked out at the blank spot where the tree once stood and realized it was the perfect place to make something I've always been intrigued to try: a big classic flower border.

The concept of an expansive flower bed packed with herbaceous perennials has its roots in English estate gardens of the early twentieth century. Herbaceous plants, instead of being necessarily classed as herbs, are species and hybrids that are adapted to return each year while their upper foliage and stems die back to the ground each winter. For a gardener to create one of these borders is to celebrate plants for their own sake. There are no other visual elements to rely on: no statuary, no fountains, no paths. This type of garden's success depends on how the plants relate to one another—and it's not easy to pull off. Even English garden designer and author Gertrude Jekyll, an early inventor of the concept, ultimately had her doubts about its practicality.

The primary popularizers of these historic estate borders, which can measure up to two-hundred-by-fifteen feet, are Jekyll and her collaborator, the Irish author and garden designer William Robinson. Both were influential tastemakers of their time with Robinson advocating the style known as wild gardening. Both promoted herbaceous perennials, including many prairie species from America like goldenrod and asters as replacements for the bedding-out of the Victorian era, a look you can still see around municipal plantings where low, bright annuals are popped in for the summer and entirely removed after frost. This was distinctly an Arts and Crafts gardening movement based on a rejection of artificiality, just as the art and decorative part of the movement rejected modern industrial technologies. Because many of these perennials (think peonies, lupines, delphiniums, and irises) bloom only for a few weeks at time, there are long stretches when they are just green leaves, or earlier in the spring, merely green shoots. This is the timing problem that Jekyll identified so honestly.

> *To have flower borders in beauty for the whole season at small cost is practically an impossibility. It can only be done by having a large reserve of plants that can be put in to replace those that have gone over, as is done in the gardens of Hampton Court. In a case where you have three separate borders, the best way would be to give each to a season, No. I to March–April–May, No. 2 to June–July, No. 3 to August–September–October.*
>
> —**Gertrude Jekyll,**
> *A Gardener's Testament* (1937)

I don't have the kind of property where I could create, much less maintain, separate garden areas to have flower beds that look interesting only for a month or two at a time. I'm not sure Jekyll ever addresses what you do in the spaces where the flowers aren't performing at their peak. Just keep them weeded without anything in bloom to draw your interest? Each area in my garden won't be blooming all out every day of the growing months, but I am trying to develop some work-arounds to keep as much of the space visually interesting for most of the growing season.

To get our long border started, we roped some close friends that were visiting over Memorial Day into helping spread eight or so inches of fresh topsoil and compost on top of the weedy ground to create a bed about thirty-four-by-nine feet. It was exciting to look at the blank slate of freshly laid soil and imagine what the possibilities could be. I knew first and foremost I wanted it to be a pollinator playground, stocked with a mix of native species and non-native plants that have open, single blossoms for easy access to nectar and pollen. And I wanted to go big, with the scale of the plantings as symphonic as a Mahler composition: full orchestra, a contralto soloist, and a double chorus.

Clearly planting a large flower border needs a lot of orchestration—like a symphony. It takes a lot of tweaking and adjusting to get the right mix with so many performers on the stage. To get the bed started as quickly as possible, I sowed handfuls of annual seeds around the bare soil that first year. Since it was late May, I added fewer of the hardy annuals like poppies and larkspurs I would've sown months before and focused on half-hardy annuals and tender perennials, such as cosmos, tall verbena, and zinnias. I planted a lot of dahlias because I knew they would be able to take over toward the end of the summer when the annuals faded. I was thrilled with the results that first season as the cosmos climbed higher and higher. By late July, the flowers were dancing like butterflies in the breeze well above my head. Overall, though, the border was a little too freewheeling. It needed some structure to anchor the exuberance of all the annuals. In my haste, I hadn't planned a color scheme. So that needed to be fixed in subsequent years. The border had a few glorious weeks and then lots of time afterward where it just looked like a green tangle of plants begging to be deadheaded. I remembered Gertrude's wise admonishment that what I was attempting was "practically an impossibility."

Now in its third year, our long border is filling in nicely. I plan to morph it into a mixed shrub border over time. I will add selections from four classes of plants that bloom at different times so a series of floral events appears over the year: a backbone of deciduous and evergreen shrubs, herbaceous perennials and biennials, bulbs, and tender perennials and annuals. The key is to incorporate shrubs with several seasons of interest to take the focus off perennials with their limited bloom times. A shrub like viburnum features spring flowers, summer leaf color, and then berries or colorful fall foliage. A successful bulb program might start in spring, with perhaps a tulip display, then transition to summer bulbs and tubers like alliums, gladiolas, and dahlias. Tender perennials grown as annuals, such as shrubby salvias, fill in the gaps between the shrubs and bulbs.

Finding discipline with color in such a big area is another big challenge. At the end of last season, the chrysanthemums finally came out with masses of blooms, but at the same time as the asters. So apricot 'Sheffield' hardy chrysanthemums bloomed alongside bright purple asters, and I'm not sure it was a winning combo. Maybe a grounding foliage color like dark eggplant or brown would pull those two together while providing a base for the other plants and flowers over the growing season. We'll see how it looks.

Another surprise in the border can be the various heights of the plants as they grow. The hydrangea shrub that wasn't as statuesque as you thought becomes obscured by the clump of zinnias that grew higher than promised in the plant catalog. This is the finessing and tweaking that's involved with the creation of such a complex enterprise as a big border. I don't think it will ever be finished—and that's just the point. It is a game of both naturalism and artifice. My long border is a laboratory. Through the intricacies of growing plants on a big scale, I'm learning on a much deeper level about new varieties to try while getting to know what might succeed. Even in its early stages, my long border has become an intricate composition of plants with an almost musical sense of texture and coloration. In this case, one that is more visual than aural.

OVERLEAF: The long border is fresh with irises and foxgloves in May and June.

OPPOSITE: Herbaceous perennials, like Jerusalem sage and coreopsis, take over the border in midsummer.

In winter, their stems stand out graphically in the snow.

FROSTED

One of the aspects I value most about living in the relative isolation of the Outer Cape is being more in tune with the natural rhythms: tides, moon phases, storm systems, bird migrations, and (most importantly for a gardener) seasonal changes. Some deceleration of the urban pace is required, but if you're able to slow down and check in with your senses, it's well worth the effort. The act of doing nothing but watching and listening is a bold choice, especially considering the stochastic way most of us consume information. That said, one day this past autumn, I must have looked away briefly from the natural cycles around me because I became the unwitting victim of what I term Seasonal Denial Syndrome or SDS.

An unseasonably warm October had me living in an SDS bubble—a second summer, where I could work outside in shorts and garden in my bare feet. I took off my sweatshirt on a late October afternoon to plant bulbs and to feel the strong sun on my back as I gardened, rinsing the dirt off my feet with the hose, unfazed by the slight chill in the water. I still picked 'Sungold' cherry tomatoes and strawberries out of the raised beds. Curious bees and other pollinators buzzed around me. I harvested a few late paprika peppers, one last white eggplant. Only a short time before, I had sown another round of Asian mustards and radishes for late autumn. Then it all changed.

One night toward the end of October, the temperature was predicted to drop into the high thirties. I said to myself, "Oh, that's not too severe. It's not freezing after all," as if I had completely forgotten how the upcoming winter worked. My SDS made me want to hold a tight grip on summer. I was still using the outdoor shower, pushing the limits of the plumbing and tempting fate (and the pipes) if an unexpected cold snap came along. My plants, however, did not forget. I had already made a few preparations for the tender ones: picking most of the lemon verbena while optimistically leaving a few out in the beds. The next morning, their once-emerald leaves had turned khaki. I neglected to pick the last of the basil (also hoping I'd get another week or so of harvest) and those plants turned into black rags. The tomatillos too. I had been hoping more of the fruits would fill out their little paper lanterns in the coming weeks, but now they dangled, dark and grotesque on the stalk, like ghouls.

My dahlias had been plugging away since August, sending out new flowers daily. They too blackened. The tall 'Blue Horizon' ageratum, which to my amazement had been blooming since June all over the garden, looked like a forgotten something in the bottom of the produce drawer on clean-out day. My once-rampant nasturtiums went from bright orange, yellow, and green to a pale dun in one night. Somehow, I thought they'd be hardier. Fortunately, I had already brought three of my precious houseplants—a Thai lime, a curry leaf plant, and an allspice tree—inside a few days earlier to keep them safe from any temperature dips below 50 degrees.

There were some survivors though. The species that can partially freeze and then shake it off once they get a hit of sunlight. Some plants have antifreeze proteins that bind to ice crystals, which inhibit them from harming the plant's tissues. I have two big, multi-year stands of parsley, and on that frosty morning their leaves were so frozen you could snap them off—but they recovered until they got hit much later in the winter. Same goes for woody herbs like sage or rosemary, frilly mustards, and kale. The chrysanthemums and asters were covered in ice crystals as well, but they later mostly bounced back. It's not easy to predict which plants will be frost hardy and which will immediately collapse, but I'm sure I'll learn over a few more winters.

The rising sun that morning revealed the real magic of frost. I walked the garden to see the different ways water was visibly frozen on the petals and leaves. Feathery ice crystals or hoarfrost clung to almost every surface. The phenomenon is rare in my experience as an inland gardener, but on the Cape, surrounded by marine moisture, it is more common. *Encyclopaedia Britannica* describes hoarfrost as "direct condensation of water vapour to ice at temperatures below freezing and occurs when air is brought to its frost point by cooling." The word derives from the adjective "hoary," meaning covered in white or gray hairs—basically, it is frozen dew.

As I studied the intricate geometry on the plants closely, I thought of Jack Frost, a character I'd almost forgotten from childhood fairy tales. He was famous for sneaking in places unannounced, creating frost ferns on windows, and generally causing mischief. With the shift from shorts weather to Jack Frost references, I realized that once again a fundamental rhythm shift had occurred. Though temperatures later went back up into the seventies, it was clear even to me that summer was over.

OVERLEAF, LEFT (*clockwise from top left*): Hoarfrost covers lamb's ears; a dahlia; Brussels sprouts; a combination of mums and salvias.

OVERLEAF, RIGHT: Hardy 'Sheffield' chrysanthemums will generally bounce back after one frosty morning.

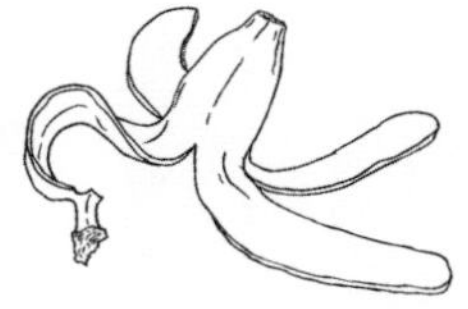

WASTE NOT, WANT NOT

My husband loves free stuff and he hates to waste anything. Sometimes I find this a bit frustrating, but deep down, I admire him for it. His level of commitment to reuse is a quality I aspire to but don't always achieve. He's that guy who saves all the bags—canvas, plastic, or paper—for future use. Our kitchen drawers have neat compartments of saved rubber bands, twist ties, corks, and those glass stoppers that come in some wine bottles. Where I might throw a torn piece of clothing away, he is expert at visible mending, where he takes clothes that are wearing out and turns a patch or a tear into something beautiful and distinctive.

He takes the same discipline into the garden. His seed-saving efforts are exhaustive. He starts in midsummer with his favorite foxgloves, roaming around the garden with a paper bag, keeping the various varieties separated as he slips the seeds off the dried stalks. He does the same with annuals like poppies, nicotiana, calendula, and larkspurs, hanging the plants to dry upside down on the screened porch (making sure the saved seeds are completely dry before putting them into storage so they don't mold). The seeds then go into glass jars that once housed mustard, pickles, jam, or sake with little hand-lettered paper labels. Did I happen to mention that he is a Virgo?

Many of the above-mentioned plants self-seed as well, often with abandon. I welcome the volunteers that pop up the following spring because most are easy to weed out or move if they are in the wrong place. We love the happy accidents that self-sowers provide: a random orlaya in the gravel, a patch of 'Pandora' poppies in the lawn next to the raised beds, larkspurs among the vegetables. Last year, Chad did his foxglove seed-cleaning on the dining table on the back terrace. This year, the terrace is covered in the biennial plants that have taken root among all the paving stones. Next year there will be a forest of tall foxglove spires I hope will be gloriously impractical to navigate.

Our property doesn't quite follow a closed-loop zero-waste rule, but we're nearing our goal and probably should just codify it into household law. Chad has us well on our way. We compost the plant material we weed, chop, or cut in various debris piles around the property. And do the same with our kitchen vegetable scraps in a composting bin. We chip brush and wood from the invasive black locust, black cherries, and bush honeysuckle that we're clearing around the edges of our property. Chad's most recent recycling project has been to build a back fence in the form of a dead hedge. This process involves setting wooden posts interspersed with branch and twig cuttings laid in loosely arranged rows that form a rough barrier. It's similar to the ancient European basket-weave fencing known as wattle—normally made of pliable willow but, in this case, the branches are thicker and not as formally arranged. The dead hedge is more of a loose pile that decomposes over time and can be replenished as branches are cleared away. Its main function, besides forming a barrier, is to create various nook and cranny homes for wildlife.

As he clears our overgrown woods, he's been keeping long straight branches to use as weaving material for the dead hedge as well as our own wattle fencing we'd like to use around the property. On many of our winter beach walks he will persuade me that we actually *can* tote that large piece of driftwood back to the car. Some of the beautifully silvered driftwood is destined for the dead hedge as posts, others are going to be used to create an outdoor shower enclosure, while smaller pieces may end up in some of his future garden sculptures.

We plan to clean up our woods a bit. It is a bit of a thicket with several non-native species, such as bush honeysuckle and black locust, we hope to weed out. Leaving some dead trees, or snags, up in the woods also creates living spaces for a variety of creatures that burrow holes in the decaying wood or take over holes from other species. Our debris piles, both large and small, offer shelter to chipmunks, frogs, salamanders, snakes, squirrels, and voles. We have brush piles where we dump plant material in an out-of-the-way spot that's too big for the compost bin. The largest is about four-by-six-feet wide. A few times, we've been startled by a large black racer snake near the pile. I've also seen it hoisting itself up into our birdbath for a drink on a hot day (they are harmless but zoom away fast; hence the name). We are also building habitat piles that are more purposefully constructed, with larger logs or branches at the bottom and smaller twigs and leaf debris on top. These more deliberate structures create multiple broader openings, almost like an apartment building for critters.

While these suggestions may seem labor-intensive, they are no more demanding than transporting the same materials to a landfill or hiring someone to get rid of them. It is such a win-win. I recommend that every gardener think about reusing instead of sending plant matter off-site. Doing so is beneficial both to the local environment and to the aesthetic appeal of your property. Using fewer store-bought fencing products and incorporating more elements that are unique to your area will also more successfully weave your property into its natural surroundings.

OVERLEAF, LEFT (*clockwise from top left*): Drying honesty, love-in-a-puff, and nigella pods. Clearing black locust branches for future projects.

OVERLEAF, RIGHT: Chad collects seeds from a clump of volunteer fennel.

LESSON

MAKING A HABITAT PILE AND A DEAD HEDGE

Habitat piles and dead hedges can vary in size depending on the dimensions of your yard or property. In an average backyard, a small pile of twigs and short branches offers shelter, while on a larger property, a habitat pile might be a few yards wide and high. Though the piles don't contain food, only brush, city dwellers might want to consider rats or mice when thinking about building their habitats.

Making a Habitat Pile

Gather the large pieces of wood, stones or discarded bricks, twigs, brush, and leaves you'll need to create the habitat pile.

- Start your pile in a quiet, out-of-the-way corner, preferably not in direct sun. Lay down larger wood pieces in a rough grid. Use stones or discarded bricks to support various chambers and openings as you position smaller twigs, brush, and leaves on top in alternating layers to create a sense of enclosure.
- Construct your habitat pile to allow more air spaces for wildlife to create living quarters. Note that this is unlike a brush pile, which is just a mound of discarded plant material.
- Feel free to refresh or reorganize the plant material once in a while if it gets too compacted waiting for the spring breeding season to end. The pile should last several years.

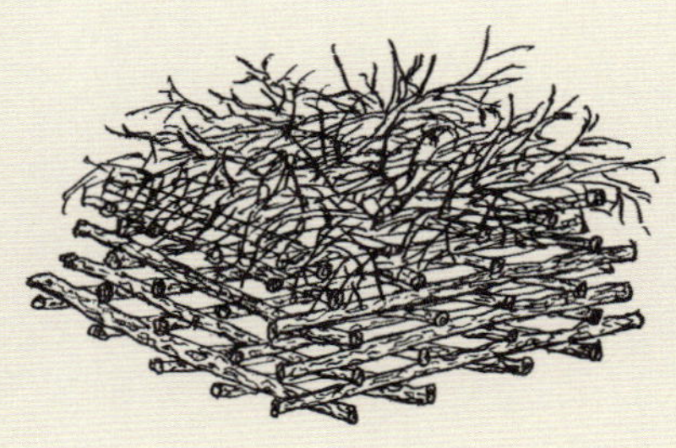

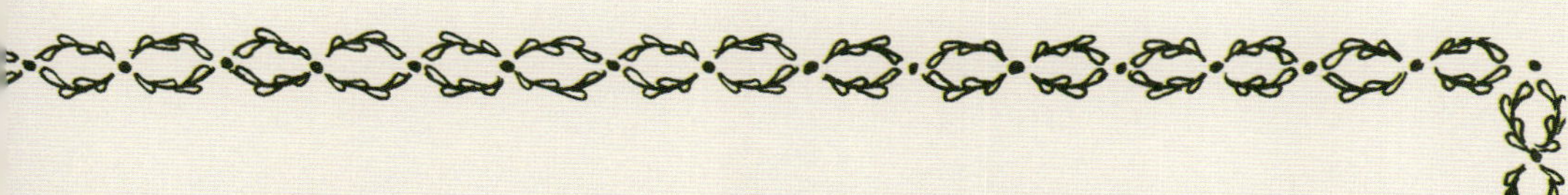

Making a Dead Hedge

Build a dead hedge where you would normally want a fence or barrier. The idea is to create a loosely woven line of branches, vines, or twigs among supporting posts. The hedge can be as short as a few feet or as long as desired.

- Mark the line of the hedge by driving rough-hewn, store-bought posts or straight-foraged branches used as posts into the ground about two feet apart. The posts can be anywhere from three to six feet tall.
- Lay larger branches in alternating layers as if you're doing a loosely woven wattle or willow fence. Place smaller branches in the same back and forth woven pattern on top. Some people build their dead hedges only with branches, while others add smaller brush and leaves on top to make it look more solid. Secure the branches with wire or string if needed, especially if the hedge is taller than three feet.
- Add more material on top each season because the hedge will biodegrade bit by bit from the bottom.
- Experiment with making the hedge more of a design feature by laying it in a curve. Or add an ornamental vine, such as clematis or hyacinth bean, to scramble over the vertical surface.

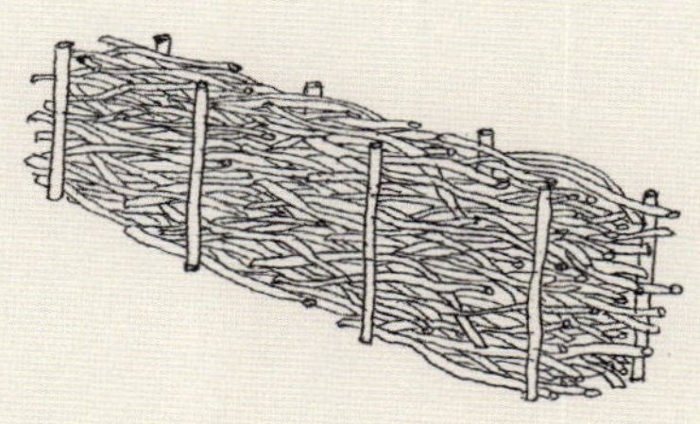

AN HERBAL LINEAGE

I have always wanted an herb garden of my own. I don't mean a garden that has some herbs in it, but a garden space designed for the aesthetic display of these useful plants. Until now, I've never had the right space. I grew herbs in my first apartment in Manhattan, but in a small window box. Since those early days, I tuck in herbs wherever I can. Later, when we moved upstairs from the fifth to the eighth floor in our New York City apartment, I moved the herbs out of their window box, which they had outgrown, and into bigger containers. Some I put in strawberry pots. Woody Mediterranean types, such as thyme and rosemary (especially the prostrate one), love to dangle out of the pottery openings as though they were perched on a cliff face above the Aegean. Given regular water, they thrived in the full sun high above the Hudson River.

I continued to grow them in containers in my shady, deer-challenged upstate New York cabin, because the soil was heavy clay, a non-draining situation most herbs hate. I was pleased to discover that the deer left their fragrant leaves alone. There seems to be a line of pungency that even the hungriest deer won't cross, but thankfully those aromatic volatile oils are the same ones that provide the flavors we love. But our limited sun was a problem in the woods, and few of the plants overwintered in our Zone 5 location, especially when the winter was wet. Herbs, like most of us, hate sitting around in the winter with wet feet.

A foursquare herb garden design allows for a little looseness with the plantings.

In Des Moines, I grew my herbs in large containers on a raised back terrace. I mixed them with salad greens, peas, and cucumbers that grew up twig supports. I had a big stand of 'African Blue' basil that was covered in bees for most of the summer. You're supposed to pinch back basil blooms to keep the plant from going to seed, but I enjoyed watching the parade of pollinators, so I let some of them go in order to always have flowers. It also seems to me that the Thai and African basil varieties don't fade after flowering like the Italian types. I also focused on tea herbs, which have been a key part of my herb plan since my Chelsea rooftop days. As a native Texan, I always have a pitcher of iced tea in the refrigerator. My blend is usually a mix of black tea or Dragon Pearl jasmine tea with a rotating mixture of herbs, such as holy basil, lavender, lemon verbena, mint, or rose geranium. For the kitchen, I grow many herbs, but my primary rotation consists of basil, lovage, marjoram, parsley, rosemary, sage, and thyme.

For if delight may provoke mens labor, what greater delight is there than to behold the earth apparelled with plants, as with a robe of embroidered worke, set with Orient pearles and garnished with great diversitie of rare and costly jewels? If this varietie and perfection of colours may affect the eie, it is such in herbs and floures.

—**John Gerard,**
***The Herball or Generall Historie of Plantes* (1597)**

Though I'd always grown herbs, I had never set aside an area where herbs were the visual focus. When we bought our place in Cape Cod, I knew there was plenty of room for one—but where? For the first two years, I followed my usual practice and sprinkled them in wherever I could. Tough, woody herbs went in the gravel garden—as many varieties of catmint, lavender, rosemary, santolina, and thyme as I could source. They thrive in our sandy, gravel conditions where most mornings they are covered with the moisture from dew from the surrounding ocean. I have been able to grow rosemary better here than

I've been able to anywhere else. Its etymology comes from two Latin words: "ros" for "dew" and "marinus" for "of the sea." Fennel and other self-seeders like basil or calendula take hold wherever they're happy, interspersing themselves in surprising spots in the gravel. "Oh really?" I remark to them while walking around the garden. "I wanted you to grow over there but now I see you like it here."

My goal was to create a dedicated space for herbs that was sunny, had well-draining soil, and was easily accessible to the kitchen. The opportunity arrived under tragic circumstances when the same early nor'easter that knocked over our silver maple ripped one set of the beautiful old garage doors off their hinges, damaging them irreparably. It was a sad day, since the doors were massively heavy and were said to be salvaged from one of the Cape's old lifesaving stations by the original owners. Luckily, we still had the other set. But during our renovation, we had transformed the spot where the right-hand doors had been into a flat shingled wall. The resulting space in front, where the doors once opened, became a sunny sheltered spot where an herb garden could go.

At about eight-by-fourteen feet, the rectangular space was ideal for my plan. I wanted a foursquare design—a traditional layout that stretches back through the Renaissance to Islam and Roman antiquity. We had bought a grindstone on a visit to the Brimfield Antique Flea Market the year before and made it the center point of two intersecting brick pathways, planted in the middle with the hardy succulent hens and chicks. Chad had found some old bricks while digging in the front yard, hidden under a thin layer of sod. We found dozens more of them in a line that once was a walkway, enough to repurpose into two new herb garden paths.

I am interested in herbs because we have a different relationship to them than we do with strictly ornamental plants. We use them to make our everyday lives better in various ways that go beyond the visual. I am also fascinated by their histories. Many of these plants were once wild but have been domesticated for thousands of years, almost like farm animals, for human utility. We pulled them from nature into our homes because we enjoy the pleasures they give us: the flavors, the scents, the health benefits. Each herb has a story to tell.

While researching my previous book, *The New American Herbal,* I read dozens of herb books, often by early-twentieth-century writers who had researched and distilled information from European sources of the late–Medieval and Tudor periods. The most famous examples of the latter are John Gerard's *The Herball* of 1597 and John Parkinson's *Theatrum Botanicum* of 1640. These are among the first books ever printed, and they include descriptions of such fantastical plants as the vegetable lamb (a plant that produced lambs instead of flowers) and the barnacle tree (a tree that bloomed barnacles that then hatched into waterfowl). These authors also promoted the Doctrine of Signatures, a popular idea of the day that outlined how each plant that is medicinally useful to humans carries a visual signature given to it by God so that we could understand its use. It was a sort of visual-based coding system where walnuts are good for the mind because their wrinkles and folds look like a brain. Carrots are good for the eyes because, when cut in horizontal slices, they look like an iris. Ginseng is a panacea because the root resembles a small human. Each plant in an herb garden of that period is a character in a drama and their lore is one of the things I like most about growing them.

American and English writers from the early part of the last century, like Helena Rutherford Ely, Eleanor Sinclair Rohde, and Rosetta Clarkson, illustrated their many books with period engravings or graphics showcasing designs of small herb gardens. My design celebrates these pasts. Though I didn't follow any from these works exactly for my own garden, I decided to keep it simple, as they did with a formal symmetrical layout and a bit of plant structure, placing an evergreen germander in each corner and a low wattle fence around the edges. My plan is inspired by my love of both Tudor herb gardens and the simple utilitarian gardens, often arranged in quadrants, of the early European colonists on the Cape. Tidy in concept, but loose and messy in the plantings—it's a forgiving approach I favor. The layout suits our late-eighteenth-century Cape Cod, and the antique bricks look right at home next to the silvered shingles on the outside of the house.

With the herbal garden nearing the end of its first year, I cut something for the kitchen almost daily. Other herbs aren't culinary or even that useful on a daily basis, but I grow them because they once were part of the herbal pharmacopeia: feverfew, motherwort, and hens and chicks (called houseleeks in the old herbals), as well as the silvery artemisias, like southernwood and wormwood. In the style of many old herb gardens, I tuck in pockets of annual blue lobelias, catmints, chocolate cosmos, gauras, ornamental sages, and pansies—both for the visual appeal and to support pollinators. I don't worry about organizing the heights too much; I want them to vary greatly, with small next to tall in the haphazard way you'd see in an engraving from an old herbal—tall bearded iris next to low chamomile, crown imperial next to creeping thyme. Once again, the formality of the foursquare design allows for a little visual chaos.

If someone told me I could only grow one group of plants—annuals, bulbs, perennials, shrubs, trees—I would choose herbs. I feel the same way about them that some folks do about dogs or cats. They are an essential part of my life and I'm so happy to finally have a place to showcase them. I love to give visitors leaves to taste or sniff as we walk the garden—the surprising fruity scent of tulsi, the astringency of wormwood, the sour tang of sorrel, the clean laundry scent of lavender, the 'Crown Princess Margareta' rose that once dawdled around and now clambers upward, covering itself in golden blossoms against the silvered cedar shingles. Pollinators buzz the horsemint and basil blossoms. And I can grab some tarragon for a chicken salad for lunch, barefoot on the brick path. That's my idea of herbal heaven.

OVERLEAF, LEFT (*clockwise from top left*): A tisane of lemon verbena; mother-of-thyme; reclaimed bricks from the former front walkway; various lavenders and sedums.

Overleaf, right: Drying tea herbs for winter storage.

Old doors often open on their own in the Cape house. "It's just the sea breezes; not ghosts," said a previous occupant.

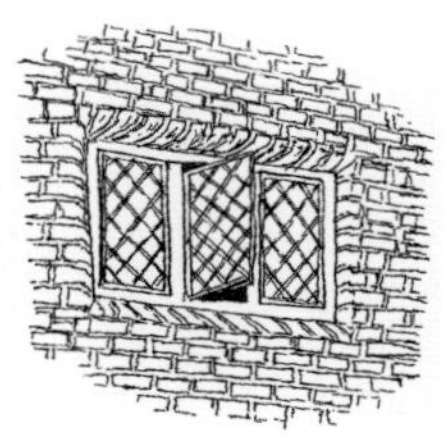

GHOSTS

Fifteen years ago, I visited Sissinghurst Castle, one of the most famous gardens in the world. Beginning in the 1930s, author Vita Sackville-West and her husband Harold Nicolson created the intricate series of garden rooms within the ruined outline of a Tudor house. Their garden has been an inspiration ever since to generations of gardenmakers, including myself, as the grounds masterfully show the English garden style of loose flowery plantings, elegantly hemmed in by strong architectural features, clipped hedges, and lots and lots of roses. To visit the garden the first time was a dream come true and, as it turned out, my dream life ended up playing a memorable part of my visit.

I was the guest of garden author Sarah Raven and her husband Adam Nicolson, Vita and Harold's grandson. Though the property has been cared for by the National Trust since 1967, Sarah and Adam's family were living there at the time. Sarah and I have worked on garden stories at various magazines, and I was the American translator for two of her garden cookbooks where I changed "auburgines" into "eggplants," "hobs" into "stoves," and "cups" into "weights." I had visited the Chelsea Flower Show to do a story, and Sarah very kindly offered to show me her own garden at nearby Perch Hill, an inspiration in its own right, before we drove over to spend the night at Sissinghurst where we roasted a chicken and cooked the vegetables we had just picked at Perch Hill hours before.

Sarah and I stayed up late talking next to the giant fireplace surrounded by generations of family mementos. I had to leave very early in the morning to head to London to catch a flight back to New

York, so when I finally went to bed around one a.m. I was exhausted. Around two a.m., I was awakened by voices, and they were agitated. It sounded like two people fighting and I thought to myself, *Are Adam and Sarah having a row in the middle of the night?* I couldn't tell where the voices were coming from, so I opened the bedroom door and looked down the staircase—nothing, no sound to be heard. I went back to sleep.

Around four a.m., I heard more voices, but this time they were more distant and definitely coming from outside my small Tudor-era window, which I had cracked open for some air before turning in. I sat up in bed and cocked my head to listen. There were multiple voices outside, and they were calling to one another in a pleasant way, not like before. In the manner one might use to summon a person to come in from outside for dinner. But it wasn't quite yet dawn. Who could be calling to one another so cheerfully in the dark? I got up to investigate, but just as I stuck my head out to look, the voices abruptly stopped as if someone had flipped a switch.

I hadn't noticed in the dark the night before that my room had a fantastic view of the iconic Tudor tower and the garden with its signature roundel of clipped yew. I noticed a shell-pink stripe of dawn starting to emerge on the horizon, brightening what was soon to be a clear blue sky. So I took my camera and headed out to the garden where I photographed for several hours. It was a perfect morning. I almost forgot about the voices until I came back in the house around eight to find everyone making breakfast. As I told my story, Sarah and Adam nodded and told me that such experiences, both auditory and visual, have been heard before among visitors to Sissinghurst.

Because the main house was destroyed centuries before Harold and Vita had bought the house, they had renovated the various outbuildings to create their living quarters as a kind of deconstructed home: kitchen over here, bedrooms over there, Vita's office at the top of the tower. All disconnected from one another. Perhaps these were the sounds of Adam's grandparents calling to his father and siblings to come in for dinner, just as one might if their "house" consisted of various buildings separated by expanses of lawn and one of the most beautiful gardens in the world. Or maybe they were the voices of some of the three thousand French soldiers who were imprisoned at Sissinghurst during the Seven Years' War in the eighteenth century. Their ghostly manifestations have been reported by visitors and staff for decades. Or maybe it was just lucid dreaming after a late dinner and too much wine?

For the record, I don't believe in ghosts. But since I was a small child, I have been an active or lucid dreamer, with many instances of sleepwalking. Though they have lessened as I've aged, sometimes I still see things while I am asleep. Quite commonly, you could hear me talking to someone who is not there. My husband reports seeing me staring blankly out of the window or into a corner, talking to someone I can see but he can't. In all these cases, I am asleep. If you talk to me, I might ignore you for a bit and then if you really press it, I will gradually wake up and not know where I am or why I'm out of bed.

The scientific term for this phenomenon, which occurs with some frequency for certain individuals (including my father and brother), is "hypnopompic hallucinations." These half-waking, half-sleeping visions or sounds occur in the period before awakening from a night's sleep, which explains why mine usually occur shortly before dawn. With regular frequency through my teens and into my forties, I would wake up to see hallucinations of people in the bedroom. Often, they were seated in a nearby chair looking at me, and usually they were speaking to me as well, though I could never hear them. Sometimes the person is dressed anachronistically. I am usually a bit afraid but never feel threatened, so I get up and walk over partially awake to the chair where the individual is seated. I can still see them as I approach and even as I put my hands through them to get them to leave. I can vividly recall the visual of their see-through bodies dissipating, almost as if I were waving away smoke.

***

Because of these occurrences, I often wonder about the previous occupants of places I've lived or visited. Not because I believe they are haunted but because I wonder if I'll have a night vision. When I lived in an old 1920s house in Des Moines, I was curious to see who might show up, but no one ever did. The house had a very warm vibration though, and people mentioned it when they visited. "Your house gives me such a homey feeling," they'd say. When we bought the Cape house, I was also curious to find out who might show up, though I knew only a bit of the house's long history.

The oldest part of our house is what is called a full Cape, meaning it is a square shingled building with two windows on each side of the front door, all anchored by a central brick chimney to protect it from nor'easters and hurricanes. It was moved in pieces (also known as "flaking") from nearby Wellfleet under the guidance of a neighbor named Thomas Blakeman. He was an artist and at one point the president of the local art museum, and he moved the house for a woman named Jeanette Jardine. He and Marion, his wife, lived a couple of doors down.

After more research, I discovered the connection between the two women in a 1918 Wellesley College yearbook. I found a photograph of Jeanette Jardine with her friend Marion Blakeman (née Hayes), our Cape Cod neighbor, a few pages away in the same class year. By the layout, we wonder if Jeanette ran our place as a boardinghouse. Marion owned a dress shop in Provincetown in the 1930s called Personal Appearance that, judging by newspaper ads from the period, also specialized in perfumes, including one of her own called Bayberry Mist. Additionally, the store sold scarves and a new stylish kind of gardening coveralls called Gardenalls. Mrs. Blakeman was a frequent subject of the local society columns for decades. "Mrs. Thomas Blakeman is heading to Boston for five days." Or "Mrs. Blakeman and her new puppy were recently seen heading to the beach on her new red Doodle Bug scooter." Jeanette seemed to stay out of the newspaper for the most part.

I would enjoy meeting Jeanette and Marion on any astral plane, but I have never experienced a ghost (or active dream) of Jeanette. I like to think about which aspects of the garden we inherited from her. The four ancient lilacs in each corner of the house with their gnarled, twisted trunks and the short yew hedges out front might have been planted by her. And the privet-edged room that encloses what is now our raised bed garden might have been her work as well as a small derelict fountain half buried by the lilies of the valley. Was it a fountain or a lily pool? It's impossible to say. The owner directly before us raised English bulldogs and there is at least one dog grave on the property with a headstone inscription that says, "When someone you love becomes a memory, the memory becomes a treasure," though it may just be a decorative monument. I plant lilies of the valley and bulbs around it.

In Jeanette's honor, I've made a flower border in the front of the house that matches the 1930s period when she would have been gardening here, filling it with lilies, larkspurs, fragrant phlox, poppies, and roses, all in pastel shades of blue, mauve, purple, and lavender. I grow old-fashioned annuals and bulbs like petunias, tuberose, and heliotrope in pots on the back terrace. I include heliotrope because it reminds me of a story I read as a child in an old book about a ghost whose manifestation is always preceded by its powdery-sweet nocturnal scent. I like to think that she might appreciate our efforts and what we've done to update, while still attending to the historical integrity of the house and its garden. Jeanette and the Blakemans were clearly interested in the eighteenth-century period because they installed historic or faux-historic hardware and interior doors to match the original nine-over-six windows. We have gone out of our way to leave as much as possible the way it was when she was here: the original cabinetry and hardware, the old windows we've had restored, and the wide-plank pine floors.

Though we have no ghosts in this house, we can tell it was always loved, over multiple generations and by many family members—and it is loved now as well. We want to keep it in good shape for the next owners to enjoy after we're gone. We will be watching from the other side, and if anyone tries to take it down to build a McMansion or something worse, we promise to be back—with a vengeance.

CETOWN, MASS.

OPPOSITE (*clockwise from top left*): The previous owner of our Cape house in her 1918 Wellesley yearbook; antique cabinetry; larkspurs in the front bed; the first bulb flowers in spring.

Cut lilacs from one of the four bushes that survive from the original 1930s plantings.

CODA

By their very nature, gardens don't survive in the same way once their creator departs—either for another house or the next life. Though the gardener leaves, the plants don't—they keep growing and changing. Sometimes a garden continues in the hands of a new gardener who will inevitably insert their own vision, even if their mission is to honor the original creative force behind the project and keep it alive. Other times, the property is abandoned or altered and nature takes over, reclaiming bit by bit the piece of land that had been borrowed.

If this sounds like a morbid note to end on, it shouldn't. Gardeners are as familiar with death as they are with life. We eventually come to realize that we only have so many years here. How many is the mystery. What you do with them is the assignment. Connecting with nature through the art and act of gardening has truly been my greatest gift. Deciding what tree to plant forces me to think, But what aspects of this tree's life will I see? Every act we complete as gardeners—planting seeds, pruning lilacs after they bloom to get larger flowers the following spring, trimming a hedge so it will grow into a better shape—is an optimistic projection into our own future selves. When we put a bulb in the ground, we are saying that when this tulip blooms for a week in spring, we plan to be here, and nowhere else, to witness it.

To garden is to enter the web of life and see it more fully. Each pollinator, each bud, each leaf that decays to straw-colored netting—they all connect us to the universe. Watching, looking, editing, digging, bending, pulling, weeding, snipping, sniffing, tasting—there is no sense left untouched. I remain full of gratitude to my parents who started me on this horticultural journey and to my husband and life partner who loves horticulture as much as I do. I am grateful for a lifetime of like-minded garden friends and fellow plant nerds who have inspired and instructed me down this garden path. My wish for all of us is simple—to see the trees we plant tower over our heads one day. But for now, we get outside and we keep gardening.

ACKNOWLEDGMENTS

To quote Mary Heaton Vorse, an author and journalist who lived in nearby Provincetown in the early part of the last century, "The art of writing is the art of applying the seat of the pants to the seat of the chair." Writing a book does require an inordinate amount of sitting and concentration. So I want to give my wholehearted appreciation to my husband Chad Jacobs for putting up with all my deadlines (those where all else in life must stop). I know it makes for a boring companion during those crunch times. You have been an unwavering source of love, support, and inspiration for forty years. I consider myself unbelievably lucky to have found an artsy, future garden lover like you in the art school at the University at Texas at Austin. It is a constant pleasure to plan and work in our garden together. Our perfect days are spent knee-deep in the flower beds with Pokey waiting patiently off to the side for us to throw his toy. Thank you for gracing this book with your beautiful drawings, which capture the right mood for the pages.

Thank you to my agent, Carla Glasser, and my editor, Angelin Adams, for your confidence in me as an author who wanted to say something new about gardening and not do a book strictly about horticulture. I know that you agree that gardens are our portal to the natural world. And the natural world is what takes us out of the everyday head of being human with all those inherent worries and concerns. To Angelin in particular, thank you for letting me be unconventional with both the content and presentation of this book and resisting the urge to put me into that well-worn box of conformity that can govern book publishing.

A big thank-you goes to the global community of gardeners and nature lovers at large. I truly believe that plant people are the best people, and I very much appreciate the authors, gardenmakers, and friends who have encouraged and motivated me, whether they knew it or not, since I first became interested in the topic in the 1980s. Like an informational sponge, I have absorbed so much knowledge and inspiration from their generosity and mentorship over the years. Everything I do or write about in my own garden is a result of their rich cross-pollination of ideas, and for that I am grateful.

I truly believe that if the world were completely made up of gardeners who sniffed flowers and dug in the soil, we would all be in much better shape.

INDEX

Clarkson Potter/Publishers
An imprint of the Crown Publishing Group
A division of Penguin Random House LLC
1745 Broadway
New York, NY 10019
clarksonpotter.com
penguinrandomhouse.com

Some of the material in these essays previously appeared in an altered form in *The Provincetown Independent.*
Photograph on page 75 by Johanna Burke.
Photograph on page 198 by Nancy Iacoi.

Library of Congress Cataloging-in-Publication Data has been applied for.

ISBN 979-8-217-03369-0
Ebook ISBN 979-8-217-03370-6

Editor: Angelin Adams | Assistant editor: Darian Keels
Designer: Yasmeen Bandoo | Production designer: Christina Self
Production editor: Terry Deal
Production and prepress manager: Kim Tyner
Compositors: Merri Ann Morrell, Zoe Tokushige
Copy editor: Ruth Anne Phillips | Proofreaders: Sigi Nacson, Michael Fedison | Indexer: Elise Hess
Publicist: Jana Branson | Marketer: Allison Renzulli

Manufactured in China

1 3 5 7 9 10 8 6 4 2

First Edition

The authorized representative in the EU for product safety and compliance is Penguin Random House Ireland, Morrison Chambers, 32 Nassau Street, Dublin D02 YH68, Ireland, https://eu-contact.penguin.ie.